Some Ways of God

C. Stacey Woods

InterVarsity Press
Downers Grove
Illinois 60515

InterVarsity Press is the book
publishing division of
Inter-Varsity Christian
Fellowship, a student movement
active on campus at hundreds
of universities, colleges and
schools of nursing. For
information about local and
regional activities, write
IVCF, 233 Langdon St.,
Madison, WI 53703.

ISBN 0-87784-715-0
Library of Congress Catalog
Card Number: 74-31843

Printed in the United
States of America

To Yvonne

CONTENTS

FOREWORD

C. Stacey Woods was born in Australia in 1909. Brought up in a Christian home, he early committed his life to the Lord Jesus Christ. Coming to America in 1930, he finished formal education at Wheaton College and Dallas Theological Seminary. At the unusually youthful age of twenty-five he was appointed General Secretary of Inter-Varsity Christian Fellowship of Canada.

In the late 1930s, groups of Christian students began mushrooming at secular colleges in the United States and soon were requesting help from the Canadian IVCF staff. A few Christian laymen in the States urged Mr. Woods to organize a similar ministry south of the border. Support flowed in and by autumn of 1940 Inter-Varsity Christian Fellowship, U.S.A., was incorporated with Stacey Woods as the founding General Secretary. He also continued to lead the Canadian fellowship until 1952.

In 1947 he pioneered yet another new movement, the International Fellowship of Evangelical Students, which was incorporated that year. For several years he led IFES and IVCF-U.S.A., both movements growing steadily in numbers of students, groups and staff.

In 1960 he resigned his U.S.A. position and in 1962, with his gracious wife Yvonne, moved again to a different nation (Switzerland), to a culture strange to them, and to new languages in order better to serve the growing worldwide family of national movements in IFES. He served this movement with distinction until his retirement in 1973.

Stacey Woods is a pioneer with large vision, unusual boldness and creativity in launching new ventures. He was God's man in launching IVCF in the States and in commencing the staff ministry of IFES. In 1967 he led in procuring a castle in Austria (Schloss Mittersill) for use by IFES as an international evangelical student conference and training center.

Few persons in this century have had as profound an influence for Jesus Christ on students and faculty at secular schools as has Stacey Woods. He understands their world, knows their problems, is familiar with a broad sweep of their literature. In evangelism he presents the gospel with clarity and power; in discipleship he proclaims the whole counsel of God, concerned for helping believers to grow steadily toward maturity in Christ Jesus.

One of his hallmarks is fervent devotion to the authority and complete trustworthiness of Scripture. Upon that reliable foundation he has contended for the historic Christian faith in a difficult arena where man's basic goodness has been assumed, human intelligence is the supreme authority and human experience the only infallible guide. Against that spirit of pragmatic relativism, Stacey Woods comes with a message from Scripture as the infallible guide revealed by our wonderful Savior and Lord.

He is a vigorous critic of pretense and cowardice, particularly of Christians who aim for popularity among fellow Christians and equivocate on moral issues to avoid controversy. If the word "prophet" can be used today, Stacey Woods surely is a prophet of

God to the college and university world. Many a local church also has benefited from his ministry.

The pages to follow breathe basic principles pertinent not only to college students but to any Christian and absolutely relevant to problems and opportunities in the *normal routine of daily life*. In addition there are gems of wisdom for Christian *leaders*. I wish every pastor, student leader, faculty member, teacher, parent and staff member would study this book and apply its message.

Our overriding concern is to glorify Christ Jesus our Lord in all that we think, say and do. But sincerity is not enough. A sincere commitment must be guided by an enlightened mind which is well-informed about God—his nature, his deeds and his *ways*. Toward this objective Stacey Woods provides us with valuable help.

John W. Alexander, President
Inter-Varsity Christian Fellowship
of the United States of America

PREFACE

After more than thirty-eight years in evangelical student work, retirement has brought changes in the pattern of my life. Naturally, I live and relive the excitement and challenge of pioneering Inter-Varsity first in Canada, then for twenty years in the United States and finally worldwide through the International Fellowship of Evangelical Students. Some of my effort undoubtedly was in the energy of the natural man. But thank God for that which has proved to be his work, about which I can humbly say with Solomon, "For thou blessest, oh Lord, and it shall be blessed for ever."

This book is a string of beads, and I hope that in this strand each reader may find a pearl or two. The chapters are a potpourri of anecdote and history, but most particularly elements of Christian truth and life that have been primary in the student ministry.

I am indebted to far more Christian friends than I can mention, to those many men and women of God whom God used to keep me treading God's straight and narrow way and to pull me back when like a foolish sheep I tended to stray. While I have referred to a few of those who have stood with me in this ministry, there are hundreds of others unnamed and unsung who as prayer partners and coun-

selors and friends shared in this worldwide student work. The years of my ministry were always essentially pioneering years. And committees with which I worked were always generous in giving me a loose and free rein. Yet student advance from 1934 on into the 1970s was never a "one-man band."

We now live in a day when technique is tending to take the place of content, when training, method and the "how-to" philosophy have become more important than what is taught. Tragically, the Christian criteria of value are now too often observable results, statistical success, rather than faithfulness to God and his Word. A sincere concern that these advertised success stories stand the test of eternity and demonstrate that in truth they are God's eternal work is often absent.

It is my earnest desire and prayer that the consciousness of the reality of the living God at work may come upon those who read this book and that they too may in measure be caught up in the ongoings of the Holy Spirit in this generation and so be used by him for Christ and his kingdom.

C. Stacey Woods
Lausanne, Switzerland

LEARNING TO TRUST GOD

1

A **Christian is called by God** to live his or her life on the principles of "trust and obey." This means that essentially he is not self-reliant but God-reliant. His value judgments and decisions are not ultimately based upon his physical sense perceptions —what he sees, hears, tastes, smells, feels—nor upon his human reason, but upon God's Word and the Holy Spirit. His final orientation is toward the unseen world of the eternal; his life is to do God's will. He lives his earthly life by faith in the living God and endeavors to think as God has revealed his thoughts in Scripture. Because he is committed to God, he relies upon God for everything. In contrast, a non-Christian does not have the living God in his thought and actions. He trusts himself or his friends and makes his decisions on the basis of his own awareness and self-centered desires as they derive from his sense perceptions plus his reason.

We should remember that living by complete trust in God is God's mandate for every Christian, not just for the exceptional Christian. Of course, the way each individual works this out in daily life will vary, depending on his circumstances and environment, but it applies equally to all the members of the church of Jesus Christ. Regardless of a Christian's profession or vocation, regardless of his wealth or poverty, this principle applies to him. If as a Christian I fail here, I shall fail almost everywhere else. Some of us with eager abandon begin our Christian lives in this way, only, as we grow older, to fall away into a life which is essentially non-Christian. Some of us discover this principle and live by it only when our years are almost spent.

An illustration of what it means to trust and obey is found in Hebrews 11:13. The writer has been considering Abel, Enoch, Noah and Abraham, men who were given certain promises by God. They believed them to be true, but more than that they stepped out and acted upon them. They did not wait for the promises to be fulfilled before acting in faith (which, of course, would otherwise not have been faith). As a matter of fact, they never lived to see and experience the fulfillment of these promises. Nevertheless, they believed God, and, consequently, they ordered their lives according to these promises. This is trust in God.

For us it means that we take seriously God's promises as set out in his Word. More than that, believing that they are true and that God cannot lie, we order our affairs on the basis of their reality. We cut ourselves loose from the principles by which secular men and women think and live. As Christians, we are different; and God has called us not merely to a divergent lifestyle but to something more profound. Our standards, value judgments, desires and ambitions—everything about us—should differ from secular man. There will be external similarities: We may wear the same kind of clothes, provided they are modest and not flamboyant. We may sleep in the same kind of bed and eat the same kind of food. Our houses may be similar. But these things should not become the distinguishing mark of a Christian.

God has called every real Christian to live a life based upon faith in him and in his various commitments to us. He has called us to trust him and him alone for everything in life.

My father was converted in Queensland, Australia, in his late teens. After completing a course in architecture, he was called by God to be an itinerant evangelist and Bible teacher. At first, he worked with an older Christian in a caravan. Later he had his own caravan and another young man as a partner in the gospel. He would go to a town, often where there was no church, set up his meeting-tent and visit the people house by house, inviting them to the services. Later, when he married, my mother traveled with him, playing a little folding organ and singing. People were converted. He would then teach them, rooting them in the Scriptures. A local church would be established with elders and deacons. Father would plan a simple building, and he and the men of the church would build it. Only then did Father feel free to move on.

Shortly after I came along, this ministry changed, especially during World War I. However, God used him to found quite a number of churches in Queensland, New South Wales and Victoria.

Father had a profound trust in God and in his promises. He took Matthew 6:33 literally: God had promised to meet his need. He never had a salary, never took up an offering for his ministry nor authorized anyone else to do so, never asked anyone for personal financial support.

This quiet confidence on the part of both my parents—for Mother stood one hundred per cent with Father—made a deep impression on me. Trusting God for everything was part of our life. My parents did not preach one thing and live another. The reverse was almost true. They lived this life of faith in God but did not talk about it.

I do not recall a time when I did not believe in God. As a consequence, I cannot quote a conversion date. In my teens I went through a brief phase of believing in evolution. Theistic evolution as a viable theory was unknown then so Father insisted I be consequential: "Well, my boy, I fully understand. Now that you are an evolutionist you are excused from family prayer and church attendance. I do not want to force you to be a hypocrite." My whole world fell apart. If materialistic evolution were true, then the God whom I had known all my life no longer existed. But I had no hope apart from him. As a family we proved his existence every day; we knew that God heard and answered prayer. To believe in a world which "just happened," apart from God who did not exist, was impossible. So my teenage excursion into evolution was short-lived.

Our family experienced times of testing. Some things that other families had we did not have—like an automobile or bicycle. But none of us ever lacked an abundance of delicious and nourishing food, more than adequate clothing and comfortable places in which to live. My sister and I had an excellent education at a time when this was exceptional. We had books, music, holidays. We never lacked any good thing; every need and more were supplied. But it was a life of day-by-day reliance upon God for everything.

Once in his caravan days Father and his fellow worker had finished up every crumb of food for breakfast. And neither of them had a cent to buy more. It came time for the midday meal. To the astonishment of the younger man, Father said, "Let us lay the table for dinner."

"But we have no food," exclaimed his companion.

"God has promised that we shall not go hungry. We must honor him by our faith in his promise."

The table was set, glasses filled with water.

"Let us sit down and give thanks for our meal," said my father. Heads were bowed and thanks returned.

As the prayer ended, a knock sounded on the caravan door. There stood a woman they had never seen before. "Me and my man are having a chicken dinner and I thought you fellers might like some." She had walked more than a quarter of a mile across the fields bringing that chicken dinner with all the "fixins."

In the early days of Inter-Varsity in the United States, when income was small and uncertain, every staff member, I think, had similar experiences. I remember one Sunday in San Francisco. Student visits in Oakland, the Bay Area and the Peninsula were finished. I had less than a dollar in my pocket—insufficient to continue south and east—and San Francisco is not a particularly hospitable city. I went to a local church for the morning service. Later I discovered my father had ministered there in evangelism for some weeks, but I knew no one. After the service a family invited me home for dinner, then to spend the rest of that day and night with them. As I left the next morning my host pressed $50 into my hand. So I went on my way rejoicing and praising God.

Sometimes I feel that Christian workers who have never really been up against it physically and materially and seen God work miraculously, though through human channels, have missed an exciting and wonderful blessing.

However, let it quickly be said that a person does not have to be destitute to live by the principle of faith in God. A millionaire who is a Christian is called to this, too. Doubtless it is more difficult for him because he has so much material security, but it is God's call nonetheless.

The trend of government is to undergird us with material securities from the cradle to the grave, providing all kinds of insurances—health, old-age, education, unemployment and so on. In addition, we insure ourselves against fire, earthquake, hurricane, accident and old-age. These safeguards are not wrong, but they can very easily become a serious hindrance to our complete trust in God. Undoubtedly, if our debts are paid and our refrigerator full, if we have money in the bank, we have the tendency to feel secure in ourselves and to sense our need of God less. Herein lies the danger.

My greatest need is to feel and know my need of God every hour. As that great gospel hymn puts it,

All the fitness he requireth
Is to feel your need of Him.

Material affluence in no respect lessens my need to rely on God. Actually, it increases it. I am in greater spiritual danger when I have plenty than when I have nothing. Hence the almost greater need of the wealthy to cry to God for mercy that they may not fail to trust him.

God warned his people Israel of this danger:

And it shall be, when the LORD thy God shall have brought thee into the land which he sware unto thy fathers, to Abraham, to Isaac, and to Jacob, to give thee great and goodly cities, which thou buildest not, and houses full of all good things, which thou filledst not, and wells digged, which thou diggedst not, vineyards and olive trees, which thou plantedst not; when thou shalt have eaten and be full; then beware lest thou forget the LORD, which brought thee forth out of the land of Egypt, from the house of bondage. (Deut. 6:10-12)

The tension between wealth and utter dependence upon God is greatly accentuated for the children of wealthy parents. Often, it seems, if children are with their parents during the period of struggle and hard work and if during this time God has been put first in the home, these children can cope spiritually with wealth. But for offspring born into great affluence, wealth becomes an enormous hazard and an almost insuperable barrier to walking with God. Well did Christ say, "With what difficulty shall they that have riches enter into the kingdom of God" (Mk. 10:23).

The essential issue, however, is not our possessions or lack of them; it is our reliance upon them or, if we are poor, our desire to have them. If we genuinely are poor in spirit, if we hunger and thirst after righteousness, then we shall know our need and in confidence turn to the living God.

Unless we can live our lives in humble dependence upon God for everything, inward and outward, which means unless we can live our lives governed moment by moment by the principle of faith in God, trusting him for all things, we simply cannot please him (Heb. 11:6).

To trust God in this way is a *simple* matter and calls for simplicity of mind and heart. But this is not to suggest it is *easy*! Constantly we must say no to the natural man with his impulses toward self-confidence, self-reliance and possessiveness, and yes to the new man, praying daily for inner spiritual renewal that we may live our days in humble trust and obedience to Jesus Christ our Lord.

KNOWLEDGE OF
THE HOLY

2

It is apparent that tremendous changes have taken place in the Western world during the last thirty years. There has been an enormous advance in scientific knowledge and its application to daily life. We live in an increasingly technological society. Generally speaking, absolute standards of ethics and morals have been abandoned for those which are relative. We have a new lifestyle. Society has become permissive and indulgent. A frightening increase in violence, cruelty, brutality and crime is deeply troubling. Relationships between men and women, husbands and wives, parents and children are no longer what they were in the 1940s. There is increasing anxiety, insecurity, frustration, even fear. Nowhere is this more true than in the English-speaking world, particularly in North America.

The evangelical Christian world has also been affected by this secular stress and change. The church has changed and it continues to change. While there has been extraordinary growth in evangelical outreach both geographically and numerically, it is open to debate whether all these changes have been for the good and whether the church today is as strong spiritually as it was thirty years ago. Certainly influenced by a permissive secular society, the evangelical church has all but abandoned any pretense of church discipline. While there has been a phenomenal growth in neighborhood Bible classes with their solid Bible study, the exposition of Scripture and solid Bible teaching is almost nonexistent. We prefer to discuss and to share rather than to listen to authoritative exposition and teaching. A jocular, folksy element has invaded our pulpits, sometimes to the point of irreverence.

Activism has become a substitute for meditation. Having become result-centered, we now tend to rely more upon secular techniques and formulas than on the mysterious, sovereign work of the Holy Spirit. Rather than depending upon the Holy Spirit and the outworking of his will as he produces his fruit, many prefer to wallow in charismatic ecstasy. We no longer truly believe in the sovereignty of God and in sovereign election by grace, even though surprisingly many still call themselves moderate Calvinists. Our hymn singing too has changed. The greatness and glory of God, his majesty and holiness, no longer is a subject of our praise. Rather, God is our friend. Sentimentally we say he is by our side. We have left almost nothing but a human Jesus. God is certainly a loving, forgiving God, but he is also a God of righteousness and stern judgment. Perhaps the whole trend in evangelical circles today may be summed up in the thought that we are losing our concept and experience of the holiness of God in our corporate worship as well as in our personal lives.

Rightly has A. W. Tozer written, "What comes into our minds when we think about God is the most important thing about us." However, with the decline of Bible teaching and exposition which cover both the Old and New Testaments, and in spite of home Bible study groups, Christians are so influenced by the decadence and relativity of secular society that less and less is their concept of God the comprehensive one revealed in Scripture. More and more it is a caricature of the most holy, the result of worldly humanistic thinking.

Fallen man naturally is an idolater. As primitive man, he makes his wood or stone idols, which represent his concept of God. Sophisticated, civilized man is not so naive, but he is equally an idolater. He does not think God's thoughts after him as they are revealed in Scripture. Rather, he bends his idolatrous concept of God to fit his relativistic, wishful thinking. His image of God is a projection of himself or his ideal self or a projection of a god he wills to believe exists, a god with a character as he desires it should be.

And so we hear on all sides, "My idea of God is such and such."

"I would not believe in a God who would permit suffering."

"In my book God will forgive and pardon every man."

And so it goes. Even evangelical Christians to a degree fall into this error, as seen in the trend toward belief in conditional immortality or universalism (regardless of the absence of any such clear teaching from Scripture) and the failure to exercise church discipline in a scriptural manner. All this is evidence of an inadequate understanding of a holy God, and his necessary judgment of sin.

Today most of us have lost the sense of awe and reverence, of fear and trembling, in the presence of God. Few of us have ever had an experience similar to Isaiah's, when he was confronted with God's holiness (Is. 6). Is it an oversimplification to suggest that our failure to comprehend, at least in some measure, the awful holiness of God is at the root of much shallow, superficial Christian faith and activity today?

There is little sense of the mystery and wonder of God's presence in our church services. All is so scheduled and programmed that it is virtually impossible for the Holy Spirit to break through and for God to reveal himself. Our cut-and-dried efficiency, with its Madison Avenue sales techniques, leaves little room for the living God. We don't even need him in order to have a successful service.

Some modern evangelists have everything so under control that three months ahead of a campaign they can predict and computerize the number of decisions and print cards accordingly. The amazing and extraordinary thing is the accuracy of these advance estimates.

The dominant characteristic of God, which pervades all his other attributes, is his ineffable holiness, his essential otherness. The root meaning of the word *holiness* conveys a sense of wholeness. This is in contrast to sin and evil, which is a form of moral sickness.

God's holiness is in part his moral excellence and perfection, his infinite purity which cannot for an instant tolerate the slightest sin. It is the holiness of God which renders it impossible for sinful man in and of himself to approach God. To quote a hymn,

Oh, how shall I whose native sphere
Is dark, whose mind is dim
Before the Ineffable appear
And on my naked spirit bear
The uncreated beam?

The absoluteness of this aspect of God's character—the white, burning, consuming light—cuts across the grain of permissive modern man and, alas, across the disposition and thought pattern of many Christians. Yet unless we, by God's grace and with the help of the Holy Spirit, recapture an understanding of God's holiness, we are doomed to continue in spiritual "shallows and flats." In spite of our feverish activity, a plethora of congresses and conventions, and all the humanistic paraphernalia of church growth methods, we will not be raised to spiritual heights.

The Old Testament is God's picture book to teach his children by visual aid and dramatic portrayal the nature of God as well as his will and provision for us. As Paul suggests in 1 Corinthians 10:11, "Now all these things happened unto them for examples, and they are written for our admonition, upon whom the ends of the world are come."

Christian young people are today almost totally ignorant of the Old Testament. I find few who can recite the Ten Commandments, God's eternal moral law. As a result, theirs is an inadequate, fragmentary concept of God. The books of Exodus and Leviticus can do more to illustrate and to educate us about the truths of God's holiness, righteousness and justice than any other part of Scripture. The Tabernacle and the law of the offerings to Jehovah are the seed bed par excellence in which to cultivate such an understanding. This type of teaching is neglected, if not sneered at, as being too fanciful to be believed. Typology is largely ignored because some have carried its meaning too far and the excesses of their imagination have resulted in a counter reaction and backlash, all to our spiritual poverty and ignorance.

My father had a large and exquisite model of the Tabernacle, built according to scale and meticulous in detail. The only detail I recall that was not correct was that although we had the ram's skins dyed red, instead of badger skins for an outer covering we had rabbit skins.

The model was set up on a large floor and was erected at an angle for better viewing. As a youngster, I greatly enjoyed helping Father set up the Tabernacle. The boards of gold were set in the sockets of silver (in this case gold and silver paint). Almost with mystery and wonder the Ark of the Covenant with its mercy seat would be reverently placed in the holy of holies and then the veil of glory and separation would be hung between the holy place and the holy of holies. Does this seem like children playing at Sunday school? I fear for many it does.

Father would lecture for as many as four weeks, six nights a week, on the Tabernacle and the offerings. Great crowds came. Many were converted. Many Christians came to an experiential understanding of the exceeding sinfulness of sin and the greatness and glory and holiness of the eternal God. Father spoke on the law of the sin offering, the provision of the red heifer, the ceremonial cleansing and above all the Day of Atonement. With bated breath I listened to the drama of that day: The crowds of people waiting. The cleansing of the high priest. The blood of atonement being carried into the holy of holies while the cloud of the Shekinah glory hovered over the Tabernacle. The tinkle of the golden bells of the high priest's robe as he came out from God's presence as atonement for the sins of that nation once more had been made.

This ancient, dramatic storybook of Exodus and Leviticus helps us to know ourselves in our innate rottenness and sin, to enter into a deeper understanding of Calvary and to catch a clear glimpse of God himself in his holiness and glory.

God will never become "the man upstairs," some sentimental Santa Claus floating on a pink cloud, benevolently patting us on the head and saying, "There, there, don't do it again." He will never be nothing more than a friend by my side who holds my hand. If I once get a glimpse of God as he really is, no longer shall I be able to sing the God-dishonoring trash that fills some of our religious hymnbooks today. I will not join with the shouting, clapping, hands-upraised, hysterical mass, who, swept into an uncontrolled emotional storm, cheer as if Christ were some over-muscled, empty-headed football hero. No, in God's presence I shall spiritually remove my shoes like Moses of old when he stood on that holy ground. I shall bow in silence before God's infinite majesty, waiting until he speaks. On the knees of my heart I will confess myself a sinner, unworthy, and humbly wait for his word of forgiveness and renewal. Never shall I carelessly rush into his presence, never make wisecracks and jokes to evoke the cackling, irreverent laugh of the ignorant crowd. Rather, my word will be "Holy, holy, holy, Lord God Almighty."

Today it is at the Lord's table, the communion service, that we are best able to understand the polarity of man's sin and God's holiness and redemption. There we should enjoy that sweet taste of sins forgiven and of God's welcome. There we should worship and adore the Most High as we are enriched in him and blessed by him.

It is fitting to close with the words of A. W. Tozer:

The gravest question before the Church is always God Himself, and the most portentive fact about any man is not what he at a given time may say or do, but what he in his deep heart conceives God to be like. We tend by a secret law of the soul to move toward our mental image of God. This is true not only of the individual Christian, but of the company of Christians that composes the Church. Always the most revealing thing about the Church is her idea of God, just as her most significant message is what she says about Him or leaves unsaid, for her silence is often more eloquent than her speech. She can never escape the self-disclosure of her witness concerning God. (Tozer, *The Knowledge of the Holy,* p. 9)

THE LORDSHIP OF CHRIST

3

A **characteristic of this generation** is an alarming increase in antinomianism, or lawlessness, in evangelical circles. The Ten Commandments, God's moral law, have been rejected as an absolute or even a normative standard of morality and ethics by the secular world. In the Christian world many Sunday schools no longer teach the Decalogue to children as God's standard of Christian living. New Testament regulations are regarded less and less as God's will for the believer and more and more as the personal opinions of Paul, Peter and John as they oscillated between Jewish tradition and Gentile mores. The pressure of a permissive society upon professedly Bible-believing ministers is tragic, for many ministers are biblically illiterate and morally and spiritually weak and many are dominated by the desire to be popular and accepted by a congregation which itself is essentially worldly and will brook no form of church discipline. Today, sadly, any form of discipline is seen as puritanical legalism.

Some time ago I had a well-known evangelical minister in my

home. In the course of conversation he mentioned quite casually that he thought most of the young people in his church lived together sexually and that there were also two or three practicing homosexuals. I asked him what he was doing about it.

His reply, "He that is without sin let him cast the first stone."

My retort, "That is irresponsible nonsense and you are derelict in your duty as a minister. What do you do about church discipline?"

His rejoinder, "That's only something Paul wrote about and he was a bachelor."

I can think of several well-known Christian organizations which for years tolerated instances of adultery and extreme drunkenness in their movement. In one case, the leader of the movement was the offender; in another, a leading member of the staff. These affairs were known yet the committee members evidently did not think they were sufficiently serious to deal with. Supinely they ignored this state of affairs. They did not want to act because action might create trouble, cause a scandal and spoil the image of the movement, which, it would appear, was of greater importance than the honor of the Lord Jesus Christ.

Some evangelicals also have a permissive antinomian attitude because of an unbiblical and exaggerated concept of the grace of God—something which the Puritans who historically magnified the grace of God never would have tolerated. The teaching runs this way: "You don't have to give up anything to become a Christian. Only believe. Move in with Christ and accept him as your Savior." Yielding to the Lordship of Christ is considered a second step taken by some people sometime after conversion. It, of course, is a desirable step, but it is optional. By simple belief salvation is eternally secured, one's future in heaven rendered certain. And, after all, does it matter so much, because ultimately all of us in the future will be made like Jesus Christ? An insistence that the acknowledgment of Jesus as Lord is an integral and necessary part of being saved is sometimes almost angrily rejected. These anti-nomians charge that this would negate salvation by grace alone through faith alone. It would be salvation by works.

This view produces an unscriptural two-tiered Christianity not too dissimilar from medieval Roman Catholic practice. Its result is a tragedy beyond words. Young people are led to believe they can continue in worldliness though Christians. Even sin, though wrong, is not too serious since it is all "under the blood." A false assurance of salvation is given to those who have believed the gospel message without ever having had a true encounter with Christ. So extreme can this teaching become that ministers will use members who openly live in sin and extreme worldly indulgence as leaders in their church.

I personally witnessed a lay leader in a fundamental church cursed by this heresy. He together with his wife would quite openly bring his mistress to church. Well-known Bible teachers would be guests in his luxurious home, shutting their eyes to both his adultery and his drunkenness. Privately they would confess that this man was not living a surrendered life but that he was safe and eternally secure. His great wealth had blinded their eyes to necessary moral judgment. This was not a case of a Christian's being suddenly overtaken in a fault and in repentance putting the sin away. This was open, deliberate defiance of God's moral law, which continued until this person's death.

All of this may appear incredible, but moral laxity, whether wrongly justified doctrinally or merely an expression of permissiveness, will increase unless the demands of a holy, just and righteous God are insisted upon and unless church discipline, done in love with a view to restore those who fail, is once more established as one of a church's normal, God-given responsibilities. Furthermore, the full gospel message must be insisted upon and boldly proclaimed—a message which includes a demand that one submit to the Lordship of Christ as part of God's free offer of salvation and eternal life.

It is important, therefore, to understand the teaching of Scripture regarding the Lordship of Christ.

In Scripture, titles and names are never empty window dressing. They are pregnant with meaning and significance. Often Old Testament names signify dominant characteristics of the bearer, for instance, *Jacob*, which means "supplanter" or "deceiver." The earthly name given to our Lord was *Jesus* or *Joshua,* foretelling his primary ministry, that of Savior and Deliverer. To some of his disciples Christ gave a new name which also spoke of their character or foretold their ministry. Simon is called *Peter*—the Rock Man. The full name and title of our divine Savior is *the Lord Jesus Christ: Lord* signifying his resurrection position, *Jesus* his earthly mission of Savior, *Christ* his role as Messiah, the anointed chosen servant of Jehovah.

Following his resurrection, the New Testament almost always gives one of these titles to the Lord Jesus, calling him either *the Lord Jesus Christ, Jesus Christ our Lord* or *Christ Jesus,* but hardly ever *Jesus* alone. Repeatedly this full title is given with reference to salvation—"Believe on the Lord Jesus Christ, and thou shalt be saved" (Acts 16:31). Was such a form of address mere empty politeness? Did it not signify position and relationship between the one coming to Christ and Christ himself?

The imperative of the Lordship of Christ in salvation is incontrovertibly set forth in Romans 10:9. Here the two essential conditions of salvation are delineated. First, if you shall confess Jesus as Lord. Surely this is a confession we make to Christ himself rather than to men, but in either case the imperative of the Lordship of Christ is clear. Second, if you will believe in your heart with all conviction and sincerity that God has raised him from the dead. In other words, this speaks of your assurance about the historic fact of Christ's bodily resurrection, the fact that Christ today is alive. Once these two conditions have been fulfilled, salvation follows. The same thought is expressed in Romans 10:13, "For whosoever shall call upon the name of the Lord shall be saved."

The statement in Philippians 2:8-9 concerning the post-crucifixion exaltation of Christ is also to the point. Here the Lordship of Christ is related to his human name *Jesus*. It is before the name of Jesus that every knee shall bow and confess him to be Lord of all. This, of course, will find its ultimate and universal fulfillment with the return of our Lord in power and glory. During this age of grace, as we trust him voluntarily, we necessarily acknowledge his Lordship as by faith we receive him. We fulfill the admonition of Psalm 2:12: Kneeling before him, in fealty with all allegiance, we submit to him, acknowledging and accepting his Lordship and sovereignty.

Two persons are not presented to us, on the one hand Jesus the Savior and on the other hand Christ the Lord. Nor is Christ some two-faced Janus or split personality. He is one, and God has declared him to be both Lord and Christ.

For man in his original state of innocence and freedom in the Garden of Eden, God was always God. Adam was given dominion over the world and its creatures, but never was he released from his moral obligation and accountability to God. In the Fall, man, asserting his free will, rebelled in disobedience, declaring, as it were, his independence from God. In so doing, he submitted himself to Satan, the devil, who became the god of this world; the kingdoms of this world became his possession. At Calvary, Christ, the last Adam, Christus Victor, as well as putting away sin by the sacrifice of himself and dying as our substitute, dealt with the cosmic issue of sin. He became victor over the world, the flesh and the devil, and by right of moral and spiritual conquest legally defeated Satan. And so this world once more became God's. God in Christ offers rebellious mankind pardon and forgiveness on the ground of repentance from sin and faith in Jesus Christ, who is now the conqueror and ruler of this world. The kingdoms of this world ultimately will be claimed by Christ after this present age of grace and opportunity for salvation is finished, and Christ will reign forever and ever.

Not only is Christ God Incarnate, but he is God's vice-regent and representative to this world. In receiving Christ, we receive God. In submitting to Christ, we submit to the Eternal One.

What is involved in repentance toward God and faith in Jesus Christ? We who are strangers, aliens, enemies now enter into a new relationship with the Father, Son and Holy Spirit; God truly becomes our God and we become his redeemed creatures as well as his children. His law and will become our rule of life. Not only are we God's children but we are members of a new race and have a new citizenship.

God has declared his Son to be Lord of the Universe. There is therefore no possible relationship with the living God unless I, his redeemed creature, acknowledge him to be my Creator and God and recognize the position he has given his Son. Christ must become my Lord and King.

To suggest that we may accept Christ as Savior without automatically submitting to him as Lord is to think of salvation apart from the Savior himself—an impossibility! It is to conceive of accepting God's gift of salvation while rejecting the Lord who is the Giver. Ruth Paxson has said it well, "There is something to be believed; there is Someone to be received." That One is Christ the Lord. It is entirely false to imagine that anyone coming to Christ may maintain his independence from the will of God in Christ Jesus and from his moral law and his holy purposes, while at the same time accepting forgiveness and reconciliation. Such a paradoxical assertion is absurd as well as contrary to Scripture.

Some say we have nothing to give up when we come to Christ. This is false. To receive Christ involves giving ourselves to him and thus becoming intimately related to him. This is why salvation, though simple, is not easy. Struggle is involved; the personal cost is high, although salvation is God's free gift of grace. To receive the gift of salvation means to receive the One who saves, the One God has declared to be Lord of all.

To suggest that such a position denies the offer of God's free grace is to misunderstand the significance of the deity of Christ, the fact of the Creator-creature relationship and the exalted position of Christ as risen and victorious. This was the original relationship of man with God. After the Fall God did not cease to be God, even though man had rebelled against him. To be born again involves the restoration of the original relationship between God and man. For converted man, God is once more his God. Hence, the truly converted person who is living in fellowship with God will daily confess to Jesus Christ, "I believe in the Lord Jesus Christ. To him I belong by creation, purchase, conquest and self-surrender. To me he belongs for all my hourly need. There is no cloud between my Lord and me. There is no difficulty inward or outward that he is not ready to meet and meet today. The Lord is my Keeper."

Apart from the Gospels the New Testament does not refer just to *Jesus* but to his full title, *Jesus Christ, Christ Jesus* or *the Lord Jesus Christ*. Isn't this significant? The exception to this is in the account of Paul's conversion. The risen and glorified Christ appeared to Paul on the road to Damascus. Paul instantly recognized this person as having supernatural divinity and cried, "Who art thou Lord?" Christ replied, using his human name alone, "I am Jesus whom thou persecutest." The Lord used his earthly name, which to Paul and other Jewish leaders was an opprobrium, while at the same time manifesting his Lordship in his supernatural appearance from heaven. Paul's conversion to Jesus the Nazarene was immediate, as was his recognition of Jesus' Lordship, indicated by his question of submission and surrender, "What wilt thou have me to do?"

Further, it is really inconceivable, if our hearts have been touched by the dying love of Christ, by the offer of himself who is salvation, that we should say to him, "Say, Jesus, I believe it's true. I'm willing to accept your gift of pardon, but I'll not give you myself. I want to run my own life. I'll come to you when I need some help and advice, but I shall determine my own lifestyle, what for me is right or wrong. I simply am not willing to accept your will and your law as my rule for life."

Of course few if any of us understand to the full the implications of the Lordship of Christ when we first put our trust in him. We do not know all that is involved nor do we understand that progressively Christ will assert his Lordship over succeeding areas of our life and that we will need to surrender daily to him and to his will. But the issue is settled implicitly when we are converted. His Lordship progressively becomes explicit as we go on with him.

Possibly there are some who wholeheartedly come to Christ without understanding the crowned rights of the Redeemer. Heart and mind are open to him but in every respect these believers are babes in Christ. This represents no unwilling heart or rebellious will refusing to obey and follow him. Such an attitude is altogether different from a person's deliberately refusing and ignoring Christ's claims.

At fault, however, is a truncated gospel message which fails to represent the true evangel. Preachers and evangelists often are so eager to be successful and to get results that they bend over backward to avoid telling any of the claims and demands of Christ. They make salvation too easy, something little more than a mild mental exercise of assent. As a result, the mortality rates following some evangelistic campaigns are horrifying.

Many years ago in the United States, Inter-Varsity had a year of evangelism with evangelistic missions, usually one week in length, held at many universities and colleges. The following year we carefully followed up the decisions. As far as we could ascertain, a little over 10% then indicated that they had been truly born again. I mentioned this result to a well-known evangelist. He simply could not believe me. He accused me of exaggeration. Then he confided to me that if 2% of those making decisions at his campaigns continued to affirm their faith he thought it was wonderful. He seemed unconcerned about the blighting, blinding effect a false, empty decision might have on the 98% who did not stand. He failed to realize the degree to which they might represent burned-over ground, and, in their turning away from Christ, a final and eternal rejection of the gospel message.

We had one week-long mission at one of the United States' most renowned universities. A famous evangelist was the speaker, and more than five hundred people made decisions that week. Six months later we made a careful check of these professed converts and could only find eleven who showed any real interest in the things of God. Yet we had tried to follow up each individual with friendship, prayer and Bible study after their decision cards had been passed on to us. Thank God for those who stood the test of time. Thank God that one of these men later joined our staff. Thank God for those who truly were born into Christ's kingdom.

Many years ago our missionary secretary was holding some special meetings with students in Toronto. At the end of one meeting four or five young men, rather angry, came up to speak with him. He had been emphasizing the claims of Christ as Lord upon every Christian, particularly in regard to foreign missionary work. They said, "We came forward to receive God at a meeting some months ago. We were assured that we did not have to give up anything to become Christians. All we had to do was believe. Now you insist that if we are Christians Christ has a claim upon us that we must seek his will for our lives. If this is true, we don't want to be Christians. We're not prepared to follow Christ in this way." They turned their backs on him and gave up all pretense of Christian faith.

What does this mean? Had they never been truly converted?

Was it a case of "many are called but few are chosen"? Or was it the result of faulty evangelism and an insufficient gospel message, in fact, "another gospel" which was not the biblical message of the grace of God?

Salvation is of the Lord. It is God's work, accomplished by his almighty wisdom and power. Not only in the person and work of the Lord Jesus Christ has the cosmic catastrophe of sin been finally and completely dealt with, but on this basis God works mightily in the sinner, raising him from the spiritual darkness and death from which he is incapable of extricating himself to a life in Christ. It is God who brings the sinner to repentance and faith. He regenerates him and imparts the divine nature to him by the Holy Spirit.

Does God do all this only to leave his redeemed child as independent as he was? A thousand times no. God brings us into his family, into fellowship with himself. Can such family life and fellowship coexist with a refusal of the Father's authority in our lives?

Finally, someone may ask, "Does this mean that once a person is born again and confesses Christ as Lord and Savior he will have no further struggle, rebellion, failure or sin?" Certainly not. But he has accepted the principle of obedience. He has recognized the authority of our heavenly Father and his Son the Lord Christ. Now he begins the process of learning, growing, conforming and becoming. And the end goal is Christ himself.

Christ's Lordship is a joyous, fulfilling servitude: "His service is perfect freedom." There should be no doubt that God's love, concern and desire for our best is sufficient power to fulfill his perfect will. Christ when on earth recognized the sovereign will of God in his life. His ultimate submission to God's will is summed up in his cry in Gethsemane—"No, not my will but thine be done." As his servants, we are no greater than he. And he has willed that, as he came into this world to do the will of the Father, even so he sends us into the world to do his will. And this involves our acceptance of his Lordship (Jn. 17:18).

KNOWING THE
WILL OF GOD

4

To know God's will is the proper concern of every obedient Christian. If a person professes to be a Christian but has no sense of inner obligation to know and to do God's will, we may well question whether he truly is a child of God. There are those who have tried to develop a foolproof formula which, when applied, will automatically indicate God's will. The difficulty with all such formulas, whether for salvation, sanctification or the knowledge of God's will, is that usually they are an oversimplification of the truth and fail to have in view the whole compass of Scripture. They are too slick.

Also, too often a neglected element in all such attempts is faith. God never sets aside the faith principle by making his will so apparent that a believer is walking totally by sight. Always the knowledge of the will of God calls for an act of faith, as in obedience we step out into what in some measure is the unknown. It is only in retrospect that we can be certain that a particular course of action was God's will. We look back and say, "Yes, truly, God led me. That decision was his will."

I am frequently nauseated by the ignorant prattle of immature Christians who speak glibly about knowing the will of God: "The Lord said this to me," "God showed his will without a doubt." Such people are egoistic, parading themselves before others as being singled out for God's special revelation. They obviously are not living on the principle of faith and seldom does their "knowledge" stand up to the scrutiny of Scripture or the test of time.

Furthermore, I have noticed how often such bland assurance is temporary. A young man is in love with a blonde. He is certain God has selected her as his life partner. He does not hesitate to broadcast this special knowledge abroad. Three months later he is traipsing about with a brunette whom he loudly announces to be God's choice for him. To attribute such weather-vane fickleness to a holy, unchanging God is blasphemy. God does not change his mind in this way.

The Bible is a book of principles which in essence are God's will and purpose for us. Sometimes these principles are spelled out in direct statement or command. Sometimes they are embedded in a parable, in the record of history or in a poem. Nonetheless, it may be said that one hundred per cent of the will of God in principle is to be found in the Word of God alone. Ignorance of the Scriptures will inevitably result in ignorance of God's will. And by the Scriptures we do not mean some scattered favorite verses or chapters but the whole of the Bible from Genesis through the Revelation.

"Well," says some aghast young Christian. "Do you mean to say I must know the whole Bible before I can know God's will?" Certainly not—for there is something, or rather Someone, provided by God to help us, namely, the Holy Spirit. He graciously accommodates himself to the fact that we may be little more than spiritual babies, and, in our Christian infancy, he comes to our aid, using our limited knowledge of Scripture to guide us. If we fail, however, to desire "the sincere milk of the Word," fail to grow in grace to

Christian manhood and womanhood, he will not always assist us and thus perpetuate our willful ignorance and retarded spiritual growth.

The two great means of grace and guidance that God has given us are the Holy Spirit and the Holy Bible. The Bible is our objective written authority, the Spirit our subjective authority. Down the running centuries the position of the church has always been to emphasize these complementary twin authorities: the Spirit and the Word, the Word and the Spirit—neither one without the other.

Our tendency, however, is to emphasize one at the expense of the other. Some Christians place almost all their emphasis upon the objective Word. They fall prey to an arid intellectualism and rationalism; they have little sense of the presence of God or the divine afflatus of the Holy Spirit. The Bible becomes their "paper pope." For others it is the subjective experience alone that counts. They rely so heavily upon the Holy Spirit that the Bible, apart from a few proof texts, becomes a neglected book. These believers have no real, operative, objective authority in their lives.

Both positions are wrong. The Holy Spirit operates through the whole Bible and the Bible serves as the objective checkpoint for all professed guidance or work of the Holy Spirit. The Holy Spirit is the ultimate author of the Scriptures. Consequently, when properly understood, the Spirit and the Word never, under any circumstances, contradict each other. Always they agree. If you tell me the Holy Spirit is leading you in a certain direction or to a certain decision, I have the right to insist that you check this out by the Scriptures. Should the teaching of Scripture be contrary to your sense of God's leading, then your inclination cannot possibly be God's will. Likewise, if all you can do is to figure out your course of action rationally and intellectually without an existential dependence upon God the Holy Spirit, yours is more likely to be a human decision than one which comes from the hand of God upon you.

Bearing in mind that the Bible is a book of principles rather than a book of particulars, how then are you led by the Spirit and the Word? Faced with an issue calling for a decision, you humbly and submissively turn to God in prayer, asking him to direct. The Holy Spirit will then use your knowledge of the Scriptures—the character of God, his plan for the church, the general outlines of his will—to lead you to an awareness of how these general principles apply to your particular question. As a Christian yielded to the will of God, your conscience and spirit will respond, and it will become clear whether or not the matter is according to the Word of God, which is his will.

Of course, for God to guide in this way, we must of necessity have a prior willingness to obey him. I remember a student at the University of Toronto coming to me for counsel about going to the Junior Prom. I first asked her, "If the Lord says no, will you obey him?"

She replied honestly, "I'm not sure."

My response was, "Please don't waste my time. The Holy Spirit is not going to waste his time indicating God's will to a person who is uncertain about the matter of obedience."

She thought for a few minutes and then said, "Yes, I will obey God."

I was then able to direct her to certain passages of Scripture. I next told her to go home and study these and pray that God would guide. God did so, and she gladly obeyed him—to her own blessing.

But what about circumstances? Doesn't God use these to make known his will? Yes, but in a secondary sense. Circumstances—open and shut doors—may serve as confirmation and illumination to a Christian who first of all is depending upon the living God and his Word. So may the counsel of older Christians. But the Spirit and the Word are God's supreme means of revealing his will.

Usually God guides in a quiet, progressive manner. But sometimes he gives a dramatic sign when great issues are at stake, as in the case of Gideon and his fleece. In my own life I recall only two such instances.

In the autumn of 1929, I was holidaying with an Australian evangelist, the late Trevor Morris, at Austinmer, New South Wales. At breakfast one morning I received the catalog and prospectus of Dallas Theological Seminary. My father had been in New York a few months previously, had met a member of the faculty, Dr. George Gill, and had told him about me. So Dr. Gill had arranged to have this information sent. My reaction was almost derisive. The thought of anyone's going to Texas to study theology seemed absurd. To train to be a cowpoke—maybe. But seminary, never! I dismissed the idea completely, not even praying about it.

Several months later I received a letter from the registrar inquiring whether I was planning to enter the seminary in the fall of 1930. Only then did I realize I had not even consulted God about his desire in this matter. As I prayed, I told the Lord that I would be willing to go for one year but that there were insurmountable obstacles. First, my parents were opposed. Next, together with Vincent Craven (later director of Pioneer Camp, Ontario) I was responsible for a work among boys, all carried on in our spare time. This involved camps, work in three large orphanages and a Friday night boys' meeting attended by hundreds of teenagers. Vincent Craven by himself could not possibly cope with all this in his spare time. And I could not leave him in the lurch.

Then a prominent Christian businessman offered to pay Vincent's salary if he would leave business and devote all his time to this boys' work. So one obstacle was removed. At that time Mother was in Bendigo, visiting her family; Father was away preaching. Each of them, unknown to the other, wrote to me that as they prayed they had the growing conviction I should go to Dallas. I, too, by this time, was sure that I should, against personal inclination, study there. So at the beginning of September, 1930, I sailed on the M. S. Aorangi for Vancouver, and went on to Dallas by train and car. I had my twenty-first birthday aboard ship.

God spoke to me similarly about entering student work. Having finished three years of theological study at Dallas, I completed university studies at Wheaton College. My plans were made. I had a ticket to India to work with Howard Guinness among English-speaking schoolboys for two or three years, then on to Australia to be ordained in the Church of England ministry in the diocese of Sydney.

About a month before I was scheduled to leave, I received a letter from the chairman of the committee of the Inter-Varsity Christian Fellowship of Canada, inviting me to become IVCF General Secretary at a salary of $100 a month. This was in 1934. I was not particularly interested in work among university students and, not liking cold weather, had no desire to go to Canada. Without praying over the matter, I replied briefly, thanking the committee for its invitation but declining the offer, pointing out that I was bound for India. A day or two afterwards I came under great conviction. It seemed as if God sternly rebuked me, saying, "You have made your own decision. You never sought my will."

In an agony of repentance I sought forgiveness. I told the Lord I did not want to go to Canada but reluctantly would do so for one year if he would clearly indicate his will. Within three days, four things happened. I received two letters, one from my father, the other from my mother. Each wrote that they had no freedom of spirit about the journey to India. They felt that mine was a fleshly decision, motivated by a desire to travel. This cast me further down. Then a cable came from Howard Guinness. Unexpectedly, he had been recalled to England, was leaving India immediately and the plans all had to be canceled. The following morning came a second letter from Canada. The committee refused to accept my no. They were convinced that it was God's will that I become the General Secretary of the Inter-Varsity of Canada. They asked me, almost ordered me, to reconsider. This time they offered me a

salary of $50 a month. So, almost like Jonah going to Nineveh, I
went to Canada in September, 1934, "for one year," and continued
as General Secretary there until the fall of 1952. This step of faith
proved to be the path of God's greatest blessing.

God seldom guides so dramatically. Usually greater exercise of
faith is called for. In these instances, God graciously used circumstances to confirm the path toward which he was urging his rather
wayward child.

For every Christian God has certain basic priorities, which
include both immediate and ultimate purposes. Unless we understand and accept these purposes and weave them into the texture
and fabric of our lives, it will be impossible to know God's will
about other matters. On the other hand, once we accept these
great, all-embracing principles, we shall find that lesser, though
important, matters will fall into place and become clear. Less
and less will we be under necessity to rush off, first to one person,
then to another, for counsel. The basic direction of our life will be
set. All other questions will resolve themselves around the fulfillment of these ultimate goals of God.

Let me mention a few of these principles:

What is God's will for me in relation to himself? That I may live
a life in which I worship him with a pure heart; that my life will be
full of gratitude and thanksgiving to him for his love and grace and
countless blessings; that I may love him with heart, mind, soul and
strength; that my life may be one of vital existential fellowship
with the Father, Son and Holy Spirit; that the basis of my life may
be faith and obedience to him in all things. Once these great goals
are accepted as priorities, anything that will hinder their fulfillment, however good it may seem to be, will be outside the realm of
God's will for me.

What is God's priority for me as a person? That day by day I may
grow spiritually and become inwardly and outwardly more like
Jesus Christ. This is God's predestination for me (Rom. 8:29).

It is also one of God's priorities that the fruit of the Spirit be produced in every Christian. This means that I shall become characterized by love, joy, peace, longsuffering, gentleness, goodness, faith, meekness, self-control. This spiritual fruit takes precedence over any gift of the Spirit, regardless of how spectacular the gift may be. In 1 Thessalonians 4:3 it is written that our sanctification is God's will for us.

Further, it is his will that we have a pilgrim heart, which means that in both heart and mind we never permit ourselves to settle down on earth as if it were our permanent home. Everything of this material existence we must regard as temporary and transitory. Our homeland and our citizenship are in heaven. It is toward heaven and eternity we journey. Under no circumstances must we allow any earthly, secular thing to rob us of the vision of the eternal city, to chain us to the standards, goods, ways or lifestyle of this earth. If we allow money, possessions, human activity or recreation, cultural pursuits, pleasure or sports, to blind us to God and eternity, we are missing one of God's top priorities for us.

God's will for me must qualify marriage plans. It is not simply that I do not marry an unbeliever, which would be flagrant disobedience and sin. I must go further and ask God to give me a partner who will encourage me and help me to realize the holy purposes God has for each of us. If these goals are accepted by each marriage partner, the couple should have little problem fulfilling God's standards and rules for the marriage relationship—in spite of women's lib. These priorities apply equally to the choice of a profession, friendship or business partnership, to recreation and every other activity we pursue. No area of life should be excluded from God's will for us.

What is God's priority for me with regard to others? That I may witness to Christ by life as well as by word; that I may teach and preach the gospel to all to whom God sends me with a view to their conversion; that I may demonstrate God's love to them by loving my neighbor as myself.

Much more could be written, but perhaps these few divine priorities will serve as basic guidelines. Once these and the other principles of God's Word are accepted and become the warp and woof of life itself, God the Holy Spirit will show us his way concerning all other details of life. But if we reject these God-given guidelines, then we are hypocrites when we talk about God's will and how we may know it.

If we hold these priorities, life will become an adventure with God, as with heart and mind we seek and commit ourselves to God's will for each day. God promises no detailed blueprint for the next ten or twenty years. He requires day by day trusting him, seeking his will, joyfully obeying him. This is the victorious Christian life.

I urge you therefore, brethren, by the mercies of God, to present your bodies a living and holy sacrifice, acceptable to God, which is your spiritual service of worship. And do not be conformed to this world, but be transformed by the renewing of your mind, that you may prove what the will of God is, that which is good and acceptable and perfect. (Rom. 12:1-2, NASV)

BY CHANCE OR BY GOD

5

*T*he book of Acts is aptly described as the Acts of the Holy Spirit. One can find no evidence of advance apostolic campaign planning for world evangelism, which is not to suggest that the Holy Spirit will not lead us in an orderly approach to our ministry. Christ stated, "I will build my church" (Mt. 16:18). The disciples understood that their task was to herald the gospel and to teach all that Christ had commanded, discipling all who believed. They witnessed that "the Lord added to the church daily those that were being saved" (Acts 2:47). They did not depend upon psychological trickery or use "human persuaders." They had no confidence in the flesh, that is, in human contrivance apart from God and his Word. Theirs was a total ministry of the New Testament revelation, not a truncated gospel limited to a simplified John 3:16.

The overall impression is that the spread of the gospel throughout the apostolic age was controlled and directed by the sovereign Holy Spirit. In fact, some of the happenings recounted in Acts simply do not make sense as good planning and strategy. Philip was in the middle of a tremendously successful evangelistic crusade in Samaria. It seems that in general the entire population was responding to the message. Yet suddenly the Holy Spirit told Philip to leave this center of great blessing and conversion and go south to the desert of Gaza where he met *one* man. Paul planned to continue his penetration of Asia with the gospel, but the Holy Spirit forbade this, and in obedience Paul went on into Europe. Little of Paul's concentration on the strategically important cities of Europe can be deduced as his grand far-reaching plan of evangelism. The fact is that Asia was Paul's plan, Europe the plan of the Holy Spirit. Undoubtedly the Holy Spirit led Paul to the strategic centers of Europe, but there is little in the book of Acts to suggest that Paul's missionary journeys were his long-range plan. Rather he wandered from place to place directed by God.

It was persecution that drove the apostles from Jerusalem, not missionary strategy or obedience. God had almost literally to knock Peter on the head, to compel him to preach the gospel to Cornelius, the Gentile. Even Paul's plan to go to Rome with the gospel was never accomplished by himself. God got him there—as a prisoner! This is not to say that there is no place for planning or prayer, but it is to assert the primacy of the sovereignty of the Holy Spirit.

If we study the work accomplished by great missionary leaders during the last 150 years, we will discover that, while there was a general vision regarding the area of the world to which God was leading, there is surprisingly little evidence either of grand strategy or of carefully planned tactics. The overall impression we get is that these missionary heroes, both men and women, followed in the steps of Abraham. In a very real sense many of them went out not knowing where they were going, nor exactly how they would live, nor in detail what they would do. The Grand Strategist was the sovereign Holy Spirit who directed these pioneers step by step as they made Christ known.

Admittedly being pioneers, they had little initial information upon which they could plan. We today are in a very different position. We have the tools and information which make advance planning possible. But herein lies a danger. In this day of the "organization man," how easy it is to set our goals, develop our strategy, perfect our technique and then bring these human blueprints to God for his blessing. In other words we can take, or try to take, the initiative from the Holy Spirit. The end result will be another example of Cain's offering. We present to God the work of our own hands—our planning. Well it has been said, "Man proposes. God disposes," for so often he sets our plans aside.

The retort may well be, "Are we never to look ahead, to discern trends and opportunities and plan accordingly?" Of course we are. But in our planning and particularly in the matter of final decision it is essential that nothing we do is even for an instant in the energy of the flesh. We must truly be led by the Holy Spirit so that all we propose and plan is in strict accord with the Scripture, both Old and New Testaments, and that we remain flexible and submissive to God, willing to scrap all our plans, to admit our mistakes in judgment and to follow blindly but in faith the leading of the Holy Spirit.

In the worldwide outreach of the International Fellowship of Evangelical Students, now working in more than ninety nations, I fear that we have grown up like Topsy. So often God was ahead of us, opening doors, establishing student witness, and we have had to scramble to catch up with him. Usually we were so busy with the work in hand that we had little time to plan for expansion into other countries.

In the late 1920s British students, members of the then young Inter-Varsity Fellowship, caught the vision of similar work in Canada, and sacrificially gave to make possible the visit of Dr. Howard Guinness to that country. This resulted in the formation of the Inter-Varsity Christian Fellowship of Canada. Subsequently

Dr. Guinness was used to pioneer similar student movements in Australia and New Zealand. At that time there was an invitation, an open door and the offer of financial support to pioneer student work in the United States, but the traditional British caution of that time regarding the United States prevented Dr. Guinness from such a venture.

It was during World War II that history repeated itself. First, students in Canada, to be followed by students in the young Inter-Varsity Christian Fellowship, U.S.A., caught the vision of student work in Latin America. Quickly they raised money for traveling expenses and urged me, then General Secretary of the movements in both countries, to make an exploratory journey. This was before the birth of the IFES in 1946-47. At that time United States citizens were forbidden to make such a journey, but, although living in the United States, I held a British passport and was under no such restriction.

Mexico was the first port of call. Visits were made to Mexico City, Pueblo, Orizaba. Conferences were held with national ministers and missionaries. Shortly after my return, Edward Pentecost was sent to Mexico, supported by North American students, to study in the University of Mexico and to pioneer El Companerismo Evangelico Estudiantil (the Mexican IVCF). Visits to the countries of Central America at that time presented no viable opportunity to commence work among students there. That was to come later.

In Colombia I visited Bogota, Medillin, Cartagena, Barranquilla. In Bogota I was entertained by the leader of the Presbyterian student work. He was at pains to persuade me that an interdenominational work was not needed. They had a full and effective program. At their weekly meetings, one week they had dancing, mainly folk dancing; another week singing and drama; another week political discussions; the fourth week a social. I asked, "What would you say is distinctively Christian about your program?"

"We always say grace at meals," was the reply. But again no open door!

From Barranquilla I was to fly to Jamaica and on to Miami. The flight was in a lumbering, eight-propeller-engine Pan-American flying boat. The water was a sheet of glass, not a breath of air. Three times we charged across the water, but were unable to become airborne. Then the captain ordered, "All passengers sit in the rear of the plane on one another's knees. We'll have one more try." I had two people on top of me. Once more we charged across the water and this time, almost with a sucking sound, the captain lifted the nose of the boat into the air and the floats finally broke loose from the surface of the water. At a very low altitude we crawled slowly about 200 miles per hour above the Caribbean, and finally, after hours of tedium, Jamaica hove in sight. But our adventure was not over.

Landing was a difficult matter. The floats or pontoons of the plane had been severely damaged, but we were able to land safely. At Pan-American expense I was put up at the now nonexistent Myrtlebank Hotel for five days. This unplanned, unscheduled layover was in God's plan and foresight, and resulted in the founding of a work both in high schools and universities throughout the British-speaking West Indies. While there I was able to visit schools, learn of the preparation for the opening of the University of the West Indies and meet with church leaders and Christians in education. They urged that we help them.

On my return to North America, the Canadian IVCF, under the auspices of the IFES, in 1948 sent Cathie Nicoll, veteran of the Canadian staff, to Kingston, Jamaica. She pioneered the Inter-School Christian Fellowship there. Later, work commenced in the new university, and since that time has spread to other universities founded later and to high schools throughout the English speaking Caribbean. Today the movement there is fully self-supporting with its own committees and staff and is able to assist the

IFES in pioneering student work in other parts of the world.

No more ironic example of God's moving ahead of us, of God taking his initiative, can be related than the extraordinary happenings in English-speaking East Africa and West Africa since World War II. After the war, the British government established a number of new universities and colleges in Sierra Leone, Ghana, Nigeria, Kenya, Uganda and further south in East Africa. Quickly the World Student Christian Federation moved to head off the possibility of the formation of any evangelical student movement in these new universities. The doctrine of ecumenical unity was proclaimed. University authorities promised not to permit a second Christian movement on their campuses. In some cases university chaplains were appointed to control student religious activity. The World Student Christian Federation sent out its own staff to Africa.

The door seemed shut fast to the IFES. But unknown or unrealized by us, God had his own strategy. He had his own "fifth column" in these same universities with their widespread campuses and impressive buildings.

As the call went out for a teaching staff for these new institutions, Christian graduates, largely from Great Britain and all formerly active in local evangelical unions, had applied and received lecturing appointments. Theirs was not merely a professional job; it was a call from God. Quite naturally they did what any other Christian lecturer or professor would have done. On a Sunday afternoon these men invited students, many of whom had had their secondary school education in missionary schools and some of whom were Christians, to their homes for a Bible exposition, or as it is known in England, a Bible "reading." This was followed by questions, discussion, prayer, tea and biscuits. Some of these students were converted. Spontaneously on their own initiative they banded together, formed Christian Unions and applied for recognition as student societies.

There was no propaganda from the outside. The IFES was never mentioned. In the face of such student initiative and responsibility, the authorities had little alternative but to grant the requested recognition. It was by this means that the PanAfrican Fellowship of Evangelical Students came into being, to be followed by national evangelical student movements in Ghana, Nigeria and elsewhere.

Attempts were made to prevent the spread of this movement, but they failed. In one instance, an Anglican bishop from England called an evangelical union together and announced to them that he was appointing a chaplain to that university college who would be responsible for their Christian activities. They were too immature and should immediately cease their prayer meetings and Bible studies. An African student quietly stood up and spoke, "Sir, you are an Englishman. We are Africans and we do not propose to be told whether we can meet to pray or to study the Scriptures on our own." The bishop had nothing further to say and hastily left the meeting.

In Edmonton at the University of Alberta, we faced a similar closed door. The university authorities permitted only the Student Christian Movement of Canada to function. While we waited and prayed without any plan by which to proceed, Father Memoriam, the Roman Catholic student priest of that university, approached us: "I favor your biblical Christianity. Please use my study for your meetings." So we began, and soon the university authorities caved in, granting this young Christian Fellowship its charter. That was in the mid-1930s, when relationships between Catholics and Protestants were very different from what they are today.

Very many other instances of this kind could be cited. The KGK (Japan Inter-Varsity) was born when a young U.S. army officer, stationed in Tokyo, Charles Hummel, later to become an IVCF staff member and for a period acting General Secretary, commenced a student Bible class in that city.

None of these beginnings was by chance. God was at work. He

was taking the initiative.

Without wishing to be pious or presumptuous, in those glorious beginning days all of us felt we were under the direction of the Holy Spirit. Ours was no spirit of expansion and empire. We loved students, longed for their spiritual well-being and that witness in the universities should be worldwide, but always with the sense that we were behind the living God, following him, entering through doors he opened. We were not concerned to be big or important. There were no quotas of converts nor achievement goals. We never had growth achievement charts for 1950, 1955, 1960, as in the business world. The IFES was, and still is, a simple, open, free fellowship of National Evangelical Unions. We are still pioneering, supported largely by student vision and sacrifice. We believe in student initiative and responsibility today as at the beginning. We still desire to follow closely behind the Holy Spirit as he moves across the face of the earth, often going beyond our plans with unexpected surprises.

My father used to say to me, "Pray that you will discern the movements of the Holy Spirit and be caught up in his ongoings, where he is working." Emphasis upon results as a justification of method is unbiblical. Just as our Lord said "My Kingdom is not of this world" (Jn. 18:36), so God's ways and means are not of this world. After all, the devil is its god. Let us remember—that which is ethically and morally wrong cannot be spiritually right.

BY MY SPIRIT

6

Since 1950 and at an accelerating tempo the chief preoccupation of many evangelical Christians has been evangelism. Along with a stress on mass evangelism, there has been a welcome emphasis upon each Christian's personal responsibility to evangelize. New approaches to people, new techniques for presenting the gospel, new ways of clinching a decision have all been calculated to help Christians become effective soul-winners.

A side effect of this emphasis, however, has been to give some people a sense of failure if they are not seeing people converted, a feeling of guilt if they are not witnessing to at least one person each day and presenting him or her with the claims of Christ. For some, a charismatic experience has proved an escape-hatch from a guilt-ridden conscience. Others have gained fresh confidence as they have taken a special soul-winning course which promises results.

Unfortunately, along with much that is a cause for thanksgiving has come an easy-believism and a presentation of a plan of salvation which fails fully to represent the entire New Testament

message, a "cheap grace," a failure to emphasize biblical repentance. The evangelist scarcely refers to the high cost of personal
commitment to Christ and, above all, to the claims of Christ as
Lord upon the one who has received him; he does not mention the
mystery of regeneration—the new birth wherein one is literally,
though spiritually, born a baby into God's family, made partaker
of the divine nature and baptized into the body of Christ by the
Holy Spirit. Soul-winning has become for many a human technique. Certain methods carry the assurance of success. All that
seems to be called for is a human decision for Christ. Of course, I
do not mean to suggest that none of those so dealt with are born
again. Thank God for those who are truly converted.

I once spoke to teenagers at a youth conference in the east-
ern United States. A part of the program was a course on soul-
winning, consisting of a few, simple, easy-to-understand steps. On
the Saturday following five days of instruction and training, the
youngsters were sent to a nearby holiday resort to witness. I was in
the back seat of a large automobile which was bringing some of
them back to camp.

"Gee, I never knew how easy it is to make Christians. I had five
decisions. How many did you get?"

"Yeah, it sure is a cinch. I got four."

And so the eager conversation ran.

A difficulty is that, while the gospel is simple, it is not all that
easy to become a Christian. These days we are told, "You don't
have to give up anything to become a Christian." This is not true.
We have to give up everything if we truly come to Christ, because
we must give him *ourselves.* "My son," Jesus says, "give me your
heart."

Salvation is *not* man's work. It is one hundred per cent God's
work, for salvation is of the Lord. It is the Holy Spirit alone who
convicts of sin. He alone opens our eyes to see and to understand
the meaning and personal significance of the gospel; he alone im-

parts the gift of faith whereby we receive Christ (Eph. 2:8). Of course it is the person himself who believes and receives Christ by an operation of his own will, but this is impossible apart from the energizing activity of the Holy Spirit.

I doubt that it is scriptural to approach anyone and everyone, and attempt to point them to Christ. If salvation is the work of God, won't the Holy Spirit lead me to speak to the one he is already preparing to receive the message? If I rush forward in human strength, am I not in danger of casting "pearls before swine" (Mt. 7:6), shocking though such words sound to our ears!

As Christians, can't we begin each day with God? In the quiet of our room we have read his Word and meditated upon it, and now we pray, "Thank you, O Lord, for your gift of another day. Here I am, your child, at your disposal, to do your will in the strength and enablement of the Holy Spirit. Fill me now afresh with the Holy Spirit. I want my feet to walk the path of your choosing, my hands to fulfill the task given me to do. I want to love people as you love them and to help and serve them. I want to speak of you to whomever you direct me. Prepare me, direct me this day that I may be your faithful witness."

In this way each day becomes an adventure with God. We are open to the Spirit's leading but only in his strength do we speak. Gone is any sense of guilt if we do not talk to several during the day. We are in God's hands to do his will. Gone is any sense of failure if we have not seen anyone come to Christ. We are his servants. Of course, if day after day presents no opportunity to witness, if we have no sense that God is using us in some way to help someone spiritually, then we should be concerned and turn in self-examination to the Lord. We must also recognize that such counsel may merely serve to get someone "off the hook" of a sense of personal obligation to speak of Christ. But this will not be the case if we are honest before God.

Furthermore, it must be emphasized that, while God calls all

Christians to be witnesses, witnessing takes a number of forms. Not all are evangelists, either personal evangelists or mass evangelists. Some are teachers; some are called upon to give comfort, to give assurance, to strengthen. God has a spiritual ministry for every Christian. The important thing is to seek it, discover it and fulfill it. The essential thing is to be spiritually prepared and ready to carry out the ministry God wants to give us. This involves the willingness to do God's will, the readiness to change our plans in order to follow the Spirit's leading.

Some years ago a young Norwegian woman who was visiting Lausanne, Switzerland, got in touch with my wife. Some of her friends had asked her to do so. My wife visited her. A few days later, just as Mrs. Woods was leaving our apartment, the telephone rang. It was the Norwegian girl. She asked, "Can I come and see you right away?" Sensing her urgency, my wife told her to come, took off her hat and coat and postponed her appointment to another day. In a few minutes the girl was at the front door. Almost the first question she asked was, "I want to become a Christian. Can you help me?" Here was a person prepared by the Holy Spirit. How dreadful it would have been if my wife had been so attached to her own plans that the girl had been put off. Incidentally, she returned to Norway, married a Christian and God has given them a splendid ministry together.

We were holidaying on the island of Elba in the Mediterranean near the west coast of Italy. One day I prayed that, in spite of the fact that there was only one Italian Protestant church on the island and we could speak only a few phrases of Italian, God would give us some ministry. The following day, together with Jonathan, our youngest son, I was working in the garden. Glancing up I noticed a girl sashaying down the road. She half smiled at me and I nodded to her and went on with my digging.

Suddenly, I heard a voice behind me, "Do you speak English?" Somewhat startled, I replied, "I think so."

Her next question was, "Can you help me?"

"I don't know. What is your trouble?"

She told a miserable tale of a dozen English students from London University, camping in a partly renovated stable which lacked basic facilities of light and water; of girls and fellows living like animals, changing sleeping partners at will.

Following the dictum that it is usually wiser for men to deal with men and women with women, I said, "If you really want help, come and talk to my wife tomorrow morning."

At supper that night I expressed a confidence that she would be back and become a Christian. My wife was more skeptical. The next morning there she was. Her first need was a hot shower. Arrangements were made for her to rent a room in Port Azzurro, the nearby village, in order to break with her friends.

She came to us several times for Bible study with my wife and a friend of my wife's. This friend, by the way, had also prayed the previous day for an opportunity, in spite of not knowing Italian, to speak to someone about her Lord. After a few days the girl confessed Christ as her Savior. A sidelight to this incident was when she said to me, "I am a student at the University of London. My roommate belongs to a Christian Union, an organization called Inter-Varsity. She was always trying to persuade me to attend their student Bible studies."

Occasionally God gives us a demonstration of his power that cannot be explained except by the supernatural. In the summer of 1949, in the early days of the International Fellowship of Evangelical Students, we were too new and ignorant to hesitate but rushed in "where angels would fear to tread." It was decided by Mlle. Raymonde Brunel (later the wife of Daniel de Benoit, our first IFES French staffworker) and myself to hold a pioneer evangelistic student camp in France at St. Brevin L'Ocean on the Atlantic coast near St. Nazaire. The IFES Executive Committee gave us its blessing. Notices were placed on bulletin boards in French universities. We prayed and waited to see who would respond.

Facilities were primitive and inadequate. Cooking was in the open air. Washing and toilet facilities were almost nonexistent. Access to the one bathroom available for girls was by means of a ladder from the street to the first floor above the ground floor and through an open window. For the men we threw together a make-shift arrangement. My wife and I with our two young sons had the one bedroom available and that was so small that we almost needed a shoehorn to get into it. We could not walk around the beds but had to climb on one to get to the other. Fortunately, during those four weeks in camp, the weather was perfect, as was the beach and the sea.

The students arrived, about fifty unconverted men and women plus perhaps twelve Christians. The first crisis arose when they discovered there were separate quarters for men and women. Quite a few had cycled to St. Brevin, sleeping together in the fields. They objected to what they called American and Anglo-Saxon morality being imposed on them. After much discussion and some humor, they agreed to this "strange segregation."

After a few days, the cook became ill. So not only did my wife and I have to shop for food, in our halting French, but my final folly was to undertake the cooking, and this for French students! Strangely, this helped me to gain acceptance. To the French it was incredible that I, the director of the camp, should stoop to do this. They were generous not only with advice and criticism but also with offers to help. And so we struggled through.

Being French, they disliked any organization or group activity. This was a camp of individualists. To my somewhat ordered mind, meals were pandemonium. Some would sing. Always there was the cry, "Histoire, histoire," and some would tell a joke, often much too earthy for our family's tender taste. Stories were often told with vivid gesture by someone standing on a table amid food and dishes.

The real crisis of that camp, however, was a virtual revolt against the Christian message—almost a refusal to listen. Meeting after meeting, speakers would face howls of derisive laughter at the mention of sin, God or salvation. Some students would shout, "There is no such thing as sin." Fortunately, the French speakers were much less perturbed by these demonstrations than I. God's man on this occasion was a French evangelist and Bible teacher named Gaston Racine. His unvarying love, sympathy and patience made some impression. But we were completely cast upon God. Unless the Holy Spirit worked, the camp would be a failure. We could do nothing. So three times a day the tiny minority of Christians almost literally cried to God that he would do what we could not possibly do. To have applied some of the new slick approaches to evangelism would have been worse than useless.

God worked and performed his miracle. It began with a student from the Middle East, a nominal Muslim who really was an atheist. He had come to the camp because he wanted to be with his girl friend, a Protestant whose evangelical commitment seemed limited to wearing a Protestant cross.

One night he could not sleep. As he tossed on his pallet, he kept asking himself, "Does God exist?" Leaving his tent he went out into the starlit night alone and cried, "God, if you are there, make me know it." Evidently he had come under conviction during the messages given twice daily.

The next morning he came to me with a smile saying, "I'm not a Christian, but now I am convinced that God exists." He asked for a Bible and commenced to read.

A day or two later, at the noon meal, he stood up and announced that he had something to say. "I am now convinced that Jesus Christ is the Son of God and that he died for my sins. I believe in him. I am a Christian."

This announcement had an electrifying effect on the camp. A spirit of seriousness and conviction came upon a number of those French students. One I remember, a big, broad-shouldered fellow with red hair and freckled face from Marseilles. He had begun theological studies, but such was the effect of his theological lecturers that he became an atheist and abandoned theology to begin anew in medicine. During some of our meetings he had been particularly disruptive, loudly proclaiming his atheism and jeering at the biblical conception of sin. It was a startling, almost shocking sight to see him alone, sitting under a tree, sobbing under the conviction of sin. This clearly was God's work, not man's. He, too, became a Christian, as did quite a number of others. Some of these the following academic year became the nucleus of "University Bible Groups" (as the movement is known in France) in several universities where previously there had been no evangelical witness.

But what of our converted Muslim student who had been studying in Montpellier? He almost forgot about his girl friend, so absorbed did he become in reading the Bible. She, poor girl, wandered about like a disconsolate wet hen. After some days, he came to me saying that he wanted to be baptized. I suggested that he wait until he returned to Montpellier and be baptized in a church. He replied, "I have never been in a church. I don't know any." What were we, an interdenominational camp, to do? After consultation with Mr. Racine and with the boy himself, we felt it of God to fulfill his request. So one sunny afternoon the entire camp assembled on the beach. We sang hymns, and Mr. Racine spoke. Quite a crowd of French holidaymakers gathered as this student was baptized in the ocean.

This witness itself produced further blessing in the camp. Our conviction clearly was that not man in his helplessness but God in the power of the Holy Spirit was at work.

A similar story could be written about a four-week training course held in Ballaigues, Vaud, Switzerland the following month. Here, too, we experienced great opposition, particularly on the part of German theological students. But here too, like Asa of old, we cried to the Lord. He heard and answered. The devil was defeated, and the result was a great step forward in the formation and growth of the Studentenmission in Deutschland, the German Inter-Varsity.

It is an enormous comfort to realize that "salvation is of the Lord." In essence it is not man's work but God's. It is not our task to convict of sin. This is the work of the Holy Spirit. He alone can illumine the mind, open the heart, motivate the will and give the gift of saving faith. Is there any greater joy on earth than to see God work in this way and to realize that he has used our feeble witness?

The evangelist Moody, it is said, was walking down the street with a friend when they passed a man drunk and lying on the sidewalk.

"Mr. Moody, isn't that one of your converts?" the friend exclaimed.

"It's evidently not one of God's," was the reply.

"As for God, his way is perfect" (Ps. 18:30).

"Thou blessest, O LORD, and it shall be blessed forever" (1 Chron. 17:27).

MATTERS OF TRUTH
AND RIGHTEOUSNESS

7

It was World War I. My father was an evangelistic chaplain posted at Camp Seymour in the State of Victoria, Australia. This was the chief embarkation point for the Australian expeditionary force. Father was there almost continuously from 1914 to 1918. A very large marquee was provided for evangelistic meetings, which were held seven nights a week. I well remember a large photograph—a sea of hundreds of men in uniform with Father standing by the center tent pole. The photo had an inscription: "To my dear wife whose sacrifice made these meetings possible."

During this period Mother, my sister and I lived in Bendigo in the home of my maternal grandfather, Mr. C. R. Stilwell, who stood in loco parentis for me during those years. My grandfather was a rather stern yet peaceful man of medium height with long white beard and moustache, ruddy cheeks and piercing blue eyes. He wore a long Prince Albert coat, his Sunday coat being trimmed with black satin, always a stiff, starched white shirt, black bow tie, gold and diamond studs. I remember seeing him without his coat only when he was chopping wood, but even then he wore his waist-coat and starched shirt. My father said he was the most just man he ever met.

Two words were never tolerated in that household—*liar* or *cheat*. When playing games if someone shouted, "You cheated," and Grandfather heard it, the game was stopped, friends sent home and I was in disgrace. To tell a lie was the greatest of all sins. To tell the truth perhaps the greatest of virtues. I remember in later years talking with Mr. Curtis, the senior master of the Stony Brook School, Long Island. "This has been a bad year," he said. "Boys no longer tell the truth. I can do anything with a boy if he tells the truth. I can do nothing with a liar."

This, of course, is the emphasis of Scripture. Lying is equated with the character of the devil, who is described as a liar from the beginning. To the contrary, God desires truth in the inward parts; the new man in Christ is admonished to speak the truth to his fellows. Christ said of himself, "I am the Truth"—which surely included more than doctrine but embraced the essence of his character as well.

The awful consequences of lying to God are illustrated in the judgment of Ananias and Sapphira, who lied to the Holy Spirit about the sale price of some property and were struck dead. In the final judgment, among those eternally cast out from God's presence will be all who love and make lies. Liars will ultimately be cast into the Lake of Fire.

Yet today little importance seems attached to telling the truth or to cheating on examinations. (A cheat is both a liar and a thief.) Christian parents often place more emphasis upon toilet training than upon truth telling. Today there are those who boast about being filled with the Holy Spirit, living the victorious life, having received "the baptism," yet who almost habitually lie and exaggerate. Exaggeration is a form of lying which may easily become an unconscious habit.

As children of the God in whom is no lie, shouldn't telling the truth be a major concern? God desires to bring us to the position where we delight to speak the truth, difficult though this sometimes is. In our witness to the unbelieving world, to be known as a person whose word is his bond is essential. Alas, this is seldom the emphasis in evangelical circles today. Rather, we are influenced by the untruthful world around us. Recently in Italy I was told, "In this country no one speaks the truth and only an ignorant person or a fool expects to hear the truth." Doubtless this is an exaggeration, but if this becomes a characteristic of a nation only judgment can follow.

Grandfather Stilwell meted out punishment with a supple strap cut at one end into eight or nine strips. It was known as "The Gentle Persuader." I well remember being caught in boyhood mischief and wrongdoing, questioned by my grandfather and then given a strapping. Once over, the issue was never again referred to, and I was in the center of a large, loving, vivacious family. Never do I remember an unfulfilled threat. Is there a more demoralizing aspect of childtraining than to threaten a punishment and fail to administer it? This is not childtraining. It is child-destruction! Today, contrary to the clear teaching of Scripture, corporal punishment in some evangelical circles is a relic of the Dark Ages, while some childtraining counselors, professing themselves to be wise, show themselves to be fools, flaunting their new insights as superior to God's eternal Word.

Justice and righteousness were the warp and woof of our life in Bendigo. Fair play, the true balance, the decision which was just for all parties, no unjust favoritism were the basis of our life together. Grandfather Stilwell was Chief Justice of the Bendigo Children's Court, and two or three days a week he heard cases and pronounced sentence, sending some boys to a reformatory or place of detention.

Bendigo in those days was full of many varieties of birds. Clouds of brilliantly colored parakeets would fly through the adjacent bushland and often into the city itself. Other gaily colored parrots, kingfishers and kookaburras abounded, as did snakes, rabbits, opossums, great lizards and other wildlife. All of us boys had a catapult, or "shanghai" as we called it, as well as a BB gun. Often we would bring down birds in sufficient numbers for a parrot pie. Because of the danger involved, the law imposed a two-mile limit beyond the city for the use of these lethal weapons.

One afternoon, after midday dinner and before returning to school, I heard the cry of a flock of parakeets outside our back gate. There they were by the dozen in the high eucalyptus trees. Dashing to my room for my shanghai, I was soon in the street shooting the birds. I had brought down a couple when I was startled by a heavy hand on my shoulders. "Now I've caught ye, and it's to Magistrate Stilwell I'm taking you."

With me quaking in my boots, an irate Irishman marched me to our front door, and in a minute I was before my grandfather. Neither of us gave any sign of recognition. Hearing the charge, my grandfather thanked my captor and said, "Leave him with me. I'll attend to the matter."

Alone, Grandfather sternly said to me, "I'll call for you after school."

The hours dragged by and at four o'clock Grandfather and Grandmother were waiting for me in the phaeton with its white fringe on top. Grandma smiled encouragement. Grandpa did not say a word. We drove to the Court House, and I followed Grandfather into the building. An attendant took charge of me and soon I was in the prisoners' dock. In a few minutes Grandfather appeared in his robes and with his gavel called the court to order. The charge against me was read. Quickly and without excuse I admitted my guilt. A stern but brief lecture followed. Sentence was pronounced, and then I was pardoned under "The First Offenders' Act." Justice had been done. My smiling grandfather, out of court, took me by the hand, and soon with Grandma we were enjoying ice cream. But never again did I break that law!

In those early years with morning and evening Bible reading and prayer, Grandfather stood almost in the place of God in my young life. I not only loved him intensely but felt a kind of joyous reverence in his presence. My first concept of God I gained from him. This is according to Scripture. When a Christian father, in this case my grandfather, properly fulfills his function, a child gains his first concept of the nature of God as Father. When a father fails to fulfill his function as true head of the home, as priest and teacher by precept and example, one of two main foundation stones is removed from the family structure. The other essential stone is the Christian wife and mother as she fulfills her God-given role.

Bendigo was a gold-mining town. Not only were there deep mines in which men would cut gold veins from the quartz, but the creeks had gold dust we could pan. Even in our back yard, after a thunderstorm had washed away a thin layer of silt, we would go out, pick up specks of gold, put them in a bottle and trade them at the local store for candy. One of my boyhood joys was to be with Mr. Neuhoffer, a German immigrant who was chief engineer at one of our greatest mines. He would take me down the mineshafts and into the building where the quartz was crushed to powder. The most exciting day each week was when the crushed quartz had been washed away and the gold was left behind to be smelted into ingots, which were to be taken by mounted police to the central gold depository. The ever-present danger of bush-rangers and armed robbery added to the thrill, although nothing so exciting occurred during my Bendigo days.

One afternoon I was walking over the mining property with my German friend when I stopped and picked up a shaft of quartz with a sizeable piece of gold embedded in it, perhaps half an ounce. Excitedly, I shouted my find to Mr. Neuhoffer.

"No, lad," he said, "it's only fool's gold—pyrites."

"No," I insisted. "It's real gold, and it's mine."

"You are right, lad; it is gold. And a good-sized nugget it is. Come, let us throw it into the hopper."

"No, it's mine," I insisted. "I found it."

"Sit down, lad, and let me talk to you. Yes, you found it. You could keep it and no one would know except we two. But God would know. This gold was found on mine property. It belongs to the mine. If you keep it, you are a thief. What do you want to do?"

"Throw it into the hopper, I guess," I said rather miserably, and so we did.

Through incidents like these, God's standards of truth, honesty, justice and righteousness were impressed upon me.

Today when cheating on examinations is so common, even among Christians and in Christian schools, I am grateful for the unwritten code of honor which prevailed in my high school. Everything depended upon the final year-end examination. Hence the pressure during exam week was terrific. To cheat on such examinations, however, was unthinkable! In all my school days I recall only one instance of cheating. The masters never knew, but we boys did. The boy was "sent to Coventry": No one spoke to that cheat for three months. So far as I know he never cheated again.

God's attributes of truth, righteousness and justice were demonstrated on earth in the life and ministry of the Lord Jesus. He never lied. No one could ever accuse him of injustice. His was a living, existential demonstration and exposition of God's character. It is God's purpose to make us inwardly and outwardly like Jesus Christ. We are predestined to be conformed to the image of God's dear Son (Rom. 8:29). Becoming like Christ should be our top priority, our greatest ambition—not service or evangelism. God is more interested in the kind of person I am than in anything I may do. If we put doing ahead of being, we fall into a tragic error.

Evangelical society in North America and the rest of the English-speaking world has become essentially activist and the question of Christian character and behavior has been pushed into the background. As a result, the church displays an increasingly low level of personal ethics and morality with its resulting loss of spiritual power. It is much simpler and easier to forget about myself as a person accountable to God, both morally and ethically, by becoming absorbed in various forms of Christian service and activity than it is to face up to the kind of person I am, my behavior and habits, and my true growth and progress as a Christian.

We need to restudy the Scriptures to understand and accept God's priorities for us, his children. Then we should give ourselves first and foremost to these divine goals. The desire of the great evangelical missionary, the apostle Paul, as he expressed it in his letter to the church of Philippi, was to lay hold of that for which Christ laid hold of him, which was to know Christ and to become like him (Phil. 3:7-12). This took precedence over his missionary activity.

Similarly, the prophet Jeremiah was led by the Holy Spirit to express this priority in these words: "But let him that glorieth glory in this, that he understandeth and knoweth me, that I am the LORD which exercise lovingkindness, judgment, and righteousness, in the earth: for in these things I delight, saith the LORD" (Jer. 9:24).

It is humbug to speak of revival and a fresh visitation of the Holy Spirit and at the same time be careless in speaking the truth, dishonest about taxes, transportation fares and paying bills, unfair or unrighteous in our dealings with others, false or untruthful in business advertising. In all of our dealings, especially within the family circle, may our yes always be yes and our no no.

CHRISTIAN CONTENTMENT

8

For thirty years, since 1945, the Western world has experienced increasing affluence, a cornucopia overflowing with the goodies of progress and plenty. But these years have also been "the winter of our discontent" as we have succumbed to the pressures of big business, fired by the forced draft of promotion and advertising.

The mass media dangle new and better products before our gluttonous eyes and make us discontented with what we have. Our present refrigerator, although entirely adequate, is no longer good enough. We need the latest automobile. Our three-year-old car is an impossibility; even the kids are complaining about our antique. All the neighbors have new models. Hemlines go up and down; ties and lapels on men's jackets are first narrow, then absurdly broad. Puppetlike we dance to the tune of avaricious designers bent on compelling us to discard perfectly good clothing in favor of the latest fashion or craze. So we become dissatisfied with what we have. Often we murmur and complain, and this is sin.

Further, not only are we goaded into discontent, but we become filled with envy and covetous desire, lusting for what others have and we do not. This also is sin.

What does it really mean when we Christians murmur and complain? First, we are saying that God does not care about us or understand our need. We begin to imagine that God does not really love us, otherwise he would fulfill our desires. How like petulant, undisciplined children we become! Because Mother or Father will not give us immediately what we want, in a tantrum we throw our toys to the floor and cry, "You don't love me."

Next, we begin to doubt God's ability to meet our supposed need. God is not sufficient. We distrust his power. We then begin to take things into our own hands. By some means we will get what God fails to give us. We no longer depend upon him.

Finally, we begin to doubt God himself. Our faith in him, our dependence upon him, wanes. Essentially by personal choice we begin to run our own daily lives in our own way.

For a Christian the focus of discontent and complaint inevitably becomes God himself, hence the severity with which God dealt with this sin in Old Testament times. In the wilderness judgment fire consumed some of the complainers among God's people (Num. 11:1). All of Israel, discontented with the manna God provided and longing for the varied diet of Egypt, particularly for meat, hurled criticism against Moses and God. Finally God sent them quail. Without pausing for thinksgiving the people rushed to kill and eat this delicacy, and "while the flesh was yet between their teeth, ere it was chewed, the wrath of the LORD was kindled against the people, and the LORD smote the people with a very great plague" (Num. 11:33). Later the same sin of complaint and murmuring again arose. The children of Israel were discontented with God's provision. This led God to punish his people by sending a plague of poisonous fiery serpents to attack them, and many died (Num. 21:6).

What is covetousness for a Christian but the desire to have more than God has provided as well as a discontent with what he has already given? The Bible has much to say to us about this all too common problem of covetousness, a motive not always apparent on the surface but an underlying drive which leads us away from God into the wilderness of unhappiness and unspoken complaint.

Three basic principles concerning the problem of discontent are found in Scripture. The first is that God loves us. He has promised that if we put him first in our lives, he will provide for our three basic physical needs: food, clothing and shelter (Mt. 6:25-33). We are given examples of this provision in nature: The flowers are beautiful without effort, far more so than any contrived attempt of man to beautify himself with the latest fashion. God feeds the birds and the animals. This world, when undisturbed by the barbarism of modern civilization's defoliating and polluting of nature, provides in abundance for every living thing under God's benevolent providence. The Holy Spirit through the Scriptures takes pains to emphasize that mankind, you and I, are of infinitely greater significance and value than lilies or sparrows. And God's punchline is this: If God in such abundance provides for the total need of flora and fauna, cannot man made in God's image likewise trust God to provide for him?

But the Bible insists that, in the light of God's undertaking and responsibility, we must rest content with the divine provision, as does all nature around us. God is sovereign in his wisdom. He endows some with more natural ability than others. Consequently, during the span of their earthly years, some may acquire more possessions than others. However, this is relatively unimportant in the light of eternity when all of us will move into a new dimension of existence, the realm of the eternal and spiritual, with a different standard of values. There the rich in this world may be poor and the poor of this world rich.

Granted, in this world there will be differences: Some will be affluent and some may be reduced to basic necessities. Our loving heavenly Father, knowing us, knows best what we need and with what we can be entrusted, and so we should be content. He asks us to trust him—his loving providence—and to be at peace. We must eschew covetousness, envy, lust, discontent. God says we have great gain if we can be content with his provision and pursue godliness, which is becoming like Christ.

The second principle concerning the problem of discontent is this: Naked we came into this world and naked we shall leave it. We cannot take anything physical, material or cultural with us. We can leave much of this as an inheritance to our children. But history is replete with examples of children being left fortunes which do nothing but send them to hell. Material riches have no intrinsic value in the perspective of eternity. Christ summed this up in his words, "What shall it profit a man, if he shall gain the whole world, and lose his own soul?" (Mk. 8:36). We might apply this to ourselves as Christians: What shall it profit us if we gain the whole world and lose our eternal reward, being saved only so as by fire? It is insanity for any Christian driven by avarice and discontent to give his time and strength for earthly material gain.

The biblical ideal, the Christian "golden mean," is this: "Give me neither poverty nor riches; feed me with food convenient for me: lest I be full, and deny thee, and say, Who is the LORD? or lest I be poor, and steal, and take the name of my God in vain" (Prov. 30:8-9).

A third principle is that a burning desire to acquire material things, if dominant, will destroy us. The love of money, the desire to acquire and possess, comes from the pit of hell. This gnawing, self-consuming lust brings about divorce within families and sends children into the "lost generation." Even if controlled to a modified degree, this materialistic ambition destroys spiritual appetite and desire.

Is this then an argument for inertia and passivity? No. The nub of the issue is the objective or direction of ambition. Is it toward self or toward God, toward myself and my family in relation to my peers or toward Christ and his kingdom?

Hence God's goal for a Christian's life on earth is contentment with what God provides plus an ambition to become more and more like the Lord Jesus. So the biblical principle governing a life of peace and contentment for a Christian on earth is this: The temporal and the material have no ultimate value or significance in view of eternity and eternal values. It is sheer madness, therefore, for Christians feverishly to pursue material goals. Rather, we should seek first Christ's kingdom and his righteousness. It is the eternal and the spiritual which are of ultimate worth. Therefore our primary investment, our property, our bank account, should be in heaven. Further, if in sincerity we give priority to eternal values which are free from a falling stockmarket, economic depression and collapse, we have eternal stocks and bonds which can never deteriorate in value and are divinely insured against any form of theft or attrition. If we put the cause of Christ first, God will care for our ultimate investment in heaven.

God, who cannot lie, promises to meet our varied needs during our earthly pilgrimage from this world to eternity. Our only discontent, therefore, should be with ourselves, our feeble, insufficient love for Christ, our failure to hunger and thirst after righteousness as we should. We should be concerned with the paucity of our investment in heaven. This is all too small in relation to what we have on earth. We need to be poor in spirit. We need to be meek and humbled by our lack of spiritual growth and accomplishment. The days of our years are far too short to be engaged in puerile trifles, the glittering tinsel of earthly things. Our supreme, our burning ambition should be eternity, and our investment should be there. God's glory, Christ's kingdom and his final revelation and vindication on earth should be our supreme desire.

What, then, in view of the ultimate reality of the new heaven, the new earth and the new humanity, should be our attitude toward the things of this life? First, all our ambitions and desires should be bounded and enclosed by what God enables and provides. We should desire nothing more and nothing different. We are assured of God's love; we are confident that he knows us, our IQ, our heredity, our environment. He knows the past, the present and the future. He knows what is going to happen in the coming days, whether there will be war or peace, prosperity or depression, hurricane or calm—everything. Knowing that he loves us, that he desires only what is best for us, we can leave ourselves and our future in his hands, content with what he provides.

Is there a better illustration of contentment with what God provides than that of Abraham after the battle of the slime pits? The king of Sodom offered him all the booty and spoil of the battle. This Abraham refused lest any should say that Abraham had become wealthy as the result of the spoils of war. He was content to have what God had provided and desired nothing beyond that. It was only after this incident that God appeared to him anew with the promise, "Fear not, Abram: I am thy shield, and thy exceeding great reward" (Gen. 15:1).

We must realize that such an attitude does not come easily or naturally. Even the apostle Paul experienced this. He had come to Rome, the goal of his longings and desires, his ultimate missionary endeavor. But he had not come as a free man, rather as a prisoner in chains. His master plan and ambitions had been frustrated. Everything according to natural thinking had gone wrong. It was thus in prison that Paul wrote to the church in Philippi, "I have learned in whatsoever state I am, therewith to be content" (Phil. 4:11). *I have learned.* This condition of divinely given rest and peace had not come suddenly. It was no precipitate charismatic impartation. No, Paul wrote from a depth of experience. *I have learned.* How many months and years of frustration, opposition and betrayal lay behind these words? How many lessons, failures and renewals? *I have learned.* As with Paul so with us: Christian contentment is part of the learning process of becoming like Christ

John the Baptist also made a narrow statement, "Be content with your wages" (Lk. 3:14), that seems to cut across the natural grain, particularly in this day of strong trade unions. This verse, like all others, must be understood in the context of the entire Scripture. Nevertheless, it also in a sense stands on its own. While we may feel called to engage in the struggle for social justice and righteousness, at the same time we must always realize that we ourselves are in the hands of a sovereign God, and regardless of the outcome of any such struggle, we personally must be garrisoned and undergirded by God's peace and the realization of the contentment of doing his will, which is always best. "Having food and raiment let us be therewith content" (1 Tim. 6:8).

Is this a counsel to inertia, to slothfulness? Is God asking that we be devoid of ambition? Are we deliberately to abandon all the zest and drive of life to succeed? A thousand times no! Scripture is plain. We are commanded "to work with [our] own hands" (1 Thess. 4:11). Even more strongly, and contrary to much current, socialistic thinking, we are commanded that "if any would not work, neither should he eat" (2 Thess. 3:10). But to struggle and to strive to have more than we need for food, clothing and shelter for ourselves, our children and the poor would seem to put us in the class of those who are driven by nervous, egoistic acquisitiveness. As a result, we fail to accept with contentment the necessities that God has provided.

Discontent can affect us in a thousand little ways. We complain about the weather, yet each day is a day given to us by God. Dare we protest when there is rain and snow instead of sunshine? In today's congested traffic, when everyone is bucking and pushing to get somewhere, a stoplight can result in the grinding of teeth and frustration. As red turns to green, irritably we step on the gas and surge forward to get ahead of the other man. Even the spiraling cost of living, together with a falling stockmarket, can drive us up the wall. We are unwilling to reduce our standard of living at the dining room table. Simplicity for us spells defeat and failure, but not so with God.

And so a habit of complaint instead of thanksgiving controls our spirit. Griping becomes our way of life. This is not to say that there is no legitimate place for criticism and agitation where honesty, truth, justice and righteousness are at stake. But usually these reactions should be on behalf of others rather than ourselves.

In moments of tension, disappointment and frustration, why not pause and count our blessings, thanking God for each one? This is no empty counsel of "the power of positive thinking" which ignores sin and evil. For ourselves personally it can be therapeutic and lead to joy and peace with the Lord Jesus himself.

Let us therefore with joy and thankfulness enter into the experience of the reality and joy of God's promise: "My God shall supply all your need according to his riches in glory by Christ Jesus" (Phil. 4:19). "And the peace [the contentment] of God, which passeth all understanding, shall keep your hearts and minds through Christ Jesus" (Phil. 4:7).

It is God's purpose and provision that while we are actively pursuing our supreme goal in this life, which is God himself, our lives should be characterized by contentment and peace with all that he has provided—accepting ourselves, accepting our situation in the world, and above all, accepting the living God himself in all his sufficiency.

THE CHRISTIAN IN A MATERIALISTIC SOCIETY

9

One of the most perplexing problems facing Christians today is how to have the right attitude toward material possessions in a materialistic society. Wealth is a relative matter. A person in modest circumstances in the Western world would be a millionaire in Bangladesh or Chad. A person in North America with an annual income of $30,000 is poor compared with the wealthy sheiks of the Middle East or the Chinese merchants of the Orient.

There are various economic theories, both personal and national. In what is a gross oversimplification, the voice of communism says, "What you have as an individual I take for the national, common good." Of course today true communism is nowhere being practiced, except perhaps in some kibbutz in Israel. The dictatorship of the proletariat has become the dictatorship of the vested few who, having clawed their way to the top, are determined to maintain control.

Socialism is another system which is unworkable because of the sinfulness of man. Socialism says, "What we have we share. While people have a right to own private property to a limited degree, national resources and means of production belong to the nation and not to any individual or cartel."

Laissez-faire capitalism has its own dictum, namely, that an individual has the right, even at the expense of others, to acquire, possess, develop, exploit, even rape, national resources. Further, a capitalist is free to reap the benefit of his individual imagination, industry and ability, and to pass on fortunes so acquired to a posterity which in many cases is indolent, indulgent, unproductive and decadent. The weakness of all such idealistic systems is man himself, who seems incapable of fulfilling the ideal.

Interestingly, economic laws in the Old Testament seem to strike a balance between socialism and capitalism. In Israel the right of private property was respected. In that agrarian society, land was the basic unit of wealth. If one man was industrious, full of ability and ambition in relation to others who were passive and idle, this man could acquire another's fields and develop them. He could have indentured labor and become wealthy while others remained poor. But he could accumulate this capital only for a period of forty-nine years. On the fiftieth year, the Jubilee, he had to return the land to its original owners and set free the indentured laborers and slaves, unless they elected personally to remain in servitude to a benevolent master.

Even during the forty-nine years of free enterprise, God-given provisions and restrictions protected the poor. Around each field a landowner was to leave a border where grain and fruit were to remain unreaped, available to the poor who could come and gather this themselves. Furthermore, during the reaping, the poor were free to glean behind the reapers, picking up fruit and grain which were dropped and left behind. But this was no free handout to the lazy. People had to work to collect it.

Great condemnation, together with God's judgment, came upon

the nation when God's economic laws were flouted and disobeyed and when the poor were exploited. These economic provisions had to do with God's earthly people Israel, for whom the land was their inheritance. But, even so, the people were not to regard the land and its produce as of ultimate value. Only the eternal God himself had ultimate value.

Today, in our materialistic society, even many Christians accept the notion that financial prosperity is an evidence of God's blessing. How often have I heard a Christian businessman say, "God has surely blessed me this year. My income has increased by $50,000." When I have asked, "How do you know that this is God's blessing? Have you considered the possibility that this is nothing but the devil's lure to beset you with money and material things so that your mind and heart turn away from God?" this question has been met with blank incredulity. To too great an extent in current Christian society material prosperity is automatically equated with God's blessing.

What should be a Christian's attitude toward affluence? To begin with, he must realize that earthly life is temporary. So many of us have a built-in sense that in spite of the death of everyone else, we shall live on and on, on earth. Death seems remote. We are unwilling to face this reality. It was not for nothing that the monks of old in their solitary cells had on their tables a human skull as a constant reminder of the transitory nature of earthly life. If we can constantly keep before us the fact that each of us is but one heartbeat from eternity, this may help us to view material things in a truer perspective.

We are but passengers on the ship of life. Our cabin may be filled, even crammed, with baggage of great temporal value, but when we arrive at our final port of call, we step off the ship with nothing of this world in our hands. All must be left behind. Only what has been invested in eternity will remain. Naked we entered this world and naked we must leave it.

A Christian must realize that material possessions have no permanent value. Supply and demand, the rise and fall of the stock market, changes in taste and fashion, the movements of society and the inevitable process of decay and obsolescence make much of what we have of temporary value. There is no security in material things. Seizure, theft, spoilage, taxation, moth, rust, all contribute to the death knell: Material things have no intrinsic, permanent value and cannot provide ultimate security.

How easily we citizens of heaven, secure in Christ Jesus, find our imagined security in earthly things! Take, for instance, the various insurances and social securities which surround and undergird us. Let me first hasten to say that there is nothing whatsoever intrinsically unchristian in these supports and guarantees which seem to cover our every need from the cradle to the grave. The danger is the effect that these securities have upon us spiritually. We feel secure against almost all of the disasters in life that can overtake us so we no longer feel with the same intensity our need of God. If my home burns down and I am out of work and there are children to feed and I have no insurances to fall back on, in an agony of desperation I will cry to God to meet my need. But with multiplied insurances, the pressure is off.

The same is true of all types of wealth. These things give us the sense of material security which is dangerous for our spiritual welfare. My greatest need is to feel and understand my need of God. "I need thee every hour" is always true and should be the constant cry of our hearts. To feel my need of God my Father and consciously to depend upon him is spiritual health. To feel secure apart from God is spiritual sickness and disaster.

It is for this reason that some Christians have found the loss of wealth and material possessions the greatest means of grace and blessing in their lives. As never before, they have been forced back upon God to trust and depend upon him.

The Bible has much to say, too, about the corroding, corrupting effects of an impatient, inordinate desire to become wealthy. Even a moderate longing to become rich can consume us like a cancer. We must follow Christ *at any cost.*

Is there a more tragic picture than that of the rich young ruler who eagerly desired to follow Christ (Lk. 10:17-22)? He had led an exemplary moral life. But the acid test of his intent came when Christ called upon him to divest himself of his great wealth, to give all to the poor and then, utterly and completely dependent upon Christ, to leave all and follow. In this case the price of discipleship was too high. Material possessions in this life meant more than Christ in this life and in eternity, and so he turned away.

The desire to be affluent applies equally to the poor as to the wealthy, sometimes more so. None of us is free from this temptation. Envy and covetousness, the burning lust to possess what others have, can sap all energy and interest in eternity. The drive to have and to hold is self-consuming, leaving no time or strength for God. When uncontrolled, this craving is self-destructive. It is the love for money and material things, that the Bible says is the root of all evil. Unchecked, unrestrained, it leads to dishonesty, embezzlement, broken homes, nervous breakdowns and suicide. Ultimately, it can destroy our souls.

The Bible is full of examples of the destructiveness of the desire for material things. Think of the story of Achan in the book of Joshua. During the sack of Jericho, he saw that beautiful Babylonian garment, the shekels of silver and the wedge of gold. He coveted them and, secretly and contrary to God's demand, he took them, hiding them in the earth under his tent. What was the result? First of all, defeat for the nation of Israel and, finally, the destruction of Achan and his family. God made him an example for his sin of disobedience and covetousness. In the New Testament we have the tragedy of Ananias and Sapphira, believers who put on a false display of Christian generosity but secretly retained a certain amount of their possessions for themselves. This dishonest desire led them to lie to the Holy Spirit as well as to the church in Jerusalem, and for this sin God slew them.

However, wealth in and of itself is not evil. It is not the possession of wealth that stands in our soul's way but the value we place upon it, in other words, our attitude toward it. It is the desire to be rich, the love of money, that is the root of all evil.

Think of the course of this world's history in relation to national ambitions for material affluence, dominance, markets and natural resources. Behind most if not all of the wars which have brought hell upon earth is the satanic lust for material dominance and control. Suffering, ruin, destruction, poverty, starvation, death— all are the consequence of war, in which no nation ultimately wins and in which only the devil counts up his gains.

What is the anatomy of the love of money on the part of a Christian? It is nothing but an unwillingness to be content with what God provides. It represents a distrust of God's goodness, a discontent with our heavenly calling.

It is no sin to be affluent, but wealth carries with it great spiritual danger to oneself and one's family. The danger to the wealthy is that they will become arrogant. Money is power, hence the Bible warns the rich against any sense of self-sufficiency, against pride and against a sense of self-attainment. The rich constantly must make the effort to find their security in God alone and not in uncertain earthly riches. They must continually trust the living God for all things, realizing that what they have is no credit to them personally but in the final analysis is God's gift.

When thou hast eaten and art *full*, then thou shalt bless the LORD thy God for the good land which he hath given thee. Beware that thou forget not the LORD thy God, in not keeping his commandments, and his judgments and his statutes, which I command thee this day: lest when thou hast eaten and art *full*, and hast built goodly houses, and dwelt therein: and when thy herds and thy flocks *multiply,* and thy silver and thy gold is

multiplied, and all that thou hast is *multiplied;* then thine heart
be lifted up, and thou forget the LORD thy God, which brought
thee forth out of the land of Egypt, from the house of bondage;
who led thee through that great and terrible wilderness, wherein were fiery serpents, and scorpions, and drought, where there
was no water; who brought thee forth water out of the rock of
flint; who fed thee in the wilderness with manna, which thy
fathers knew not, that he might humble thee, and that he might
prove thee, to do thee good at thy latter end; and thou say in
thine heart, *My* power and the might of *mine* hand hath gotten
me this wealth. But thou shalt remember the LORD thy God: for
it is *he that giveth thee power to get wealth,* that he may establish
his covenant which he sware unto thy fathers, as it is this day.
(Deut. 8:10-18)

We are stewards of what God has given and are accountable to
him for the use of this wealth. Rather than being characterized by
ostentatious luxury and an affluent lifestyle, we should be modest
and frugal and above all should be rich in good works, using what
we have for the cause of Christ and the needs of humanity.

Ideally, every Christian family should set a standard of living
which embraces home, food, clothing, recreation and all the necessary amenities of life. The children's education, their health and
their relation to their peers should all be considered. But once we
have set this standard, as our riches increase our standard of living
should not rise; instead, our Christian stewardship should increase. Those who are relatively poor should honor the godly rich
who live on this basis and benefit by their example.

The Christian poor have their own particular temptations
in a materialistic society. They can see the three cars in the drive-
way, the extra summer home, the frequent trips abroad, together
with the spectacle of unjustifiable wastage. It is not easy to see all
this and not be envious and bitter. Yet the best things of life are
free. We can school ourselves in the simple joys of walking through

parks and woodlands, learning to watch the birds and the little animals, enjoying the sunrise and sunset. These are God's free bounty to everyone. As we enjoy them, they can free us from envy, even if we ourselves have a very simple but adequate standard of living. Above all, we must not cast envious eyes upon others, wanting what they have.

There is also the insoluble problem of the hungry and depressed millions who are starving to death. Even though they are remote from us, we have a responsibility to help them.

A difficulty is that so many organizations purporting to meet these needs fatten themselves on sacrificial donations by excessive administrative costs, extravagant travel allowances, and fantastically high salaries and overheads, so that only a small percentage of the money contributed to the needy actually goes to their relief. There are, however, a few societies which operate on an economical and ethical basis. Care should be taken to investigate what percentage of each dollar actually goes to the cause intended. One exemplary mission has two funds, one for missions and relief work, in which every cent of every donated dollar is sent abroad, a second to cover administrative costs. These two are kept entirely separate so that a donor can know exactly how his money is being used.

A Christian philosophy of life in a materialistic society may be summed up in the words of our Lord, which he quoted from the Old Testament, "Man shall not live by bread alone but by every word that proceedeth out of the mouth of God" (Mt. 4:4). Yes, we *need* food, clothing and shelter in sufficiency, but none of us *needs* luxury. Once our priorities are in the right order so that the eternal and spiritual take first place, then everything else will fall into its God-ordained order. We shall live our lives in this world as human beings, but also as God's children, facing eternity. Then God will guide us, bless us and help us to live that life that pleases him.

Money is a good servant, but a bad master. Use it as a tool for God's kingdom.

"OURSELVES YOUR SERVANTS," OR LEADERS AND FOLLOWERS

10

Great attention is being paid these days, at every level of Christian activity, to the development of leaders. Were there ever more training courses on Christian leadership? I sometimes wonder if the evangelical world is not in danger of producing more generals than foot soldiers.

The danger, however, is that too often the criteria of leadership seem to be limited to natural qualifications and training plus a confession of Christ, together with a zeal for evangelism, church planting and missionary work. Insufficient thought and attention is given to spiritual and biblical qualifications, such as the requirements for an elder described in 1 Timothy, Titus and 1 Peter.

Bishop Taylor-Smith, Chaplain General of the British forces in World War I, some years ago was speaking at Canadian Keswick. I was with him, serving as a kind of honorary chaplain. My duties were to shield him from unnecessary visitors, to take care of his appointments and reservations, to help him dress, to accompany him to meetings and generally to be his "man Friday." Those days were a time of tremendous joy and fellowship, and I learned much.

The popular event of those days was to witness the portly bishop's swim each afternoon. Crowds would line the dock to the annoyance and embarrassment of the Keswick director, the late Roland V. Bingham, who was busy censoring the size of swimming suits. The corpulent bishop, with stately Episcopal gait, would walk to the end of the diving board, turn around and face the crowd, and then solemnly perform a perfect back flip into the lake to the gasps of the admiring females.

After breakfast one morning the bishop and I were walking in the flower garden. Suddenly a bustling little man obviously consumed with his own importance hurried up to the bishop with outstretched hands. With a winning smile, he eagerly grasped the hand of the bishop: "I'm ——— ———. And I am now the head of the Missionary Society."

"Well, well, well," beamed Bishop Taylor-Smith. "I am a flower pot."

The young man dropped his hand. His eyes seemed to glaze over as his mouth sagged open. He was convinced that the poor bishop's mind had suddenly become unhinged.

Unperturbed, the bishop continued, "Yes, yes, I'm a flower pot. You know what you do with flower pots, don't you? You plant seedlings in them. So you are the head of the Missionary Society. Splendid. Now do plant a seedling. Tell me how I may become a Christian."

Confused more than ever, the wretched young man, now completely deflated, mumbled something about being in a hurry and dashed away, while we quietly continued our walk.

Over and over the bishop offered this sort of challenge when he was Chaplain General. Often when interviewing a candidate for the chaplaincy he would take out his watch and say, "I am a wounded soldier dying in the field of battle. I have three minutes to live. Tell me how I may become a Christian." The correct answer to this question was a key qualification for a chaplain's appointment.

Personal ambition, the desire for recognition, position or leadership, the drive to be famous, personally successful or prominent, is quite contrary to New Testament teaching. How many frustrated but ambitious wives have schemed to propel a reluctant husband into organizational prominence, sometimes beyond his God-given capacity, in order to fulfill vicariously their own desire to be prominent. So often the end result has been tragedy.

In the case of children, an ambitious, activist parent can do much harm. The youngster may play the piano or the clarinet. And so we hear:

"My son plays the piano beautifully."

"You should hear Johnny. He's terrific on the clarinet."

Perhaps influenced by the Hollywood of a generation ago, the aspiration of some parents is that their children may become starlets in an evangelical astrodome. For most youngsters, this is thoroughly bad. Many have not yet reached the stage of conscious accountability to God as against the self-serving encouraged by the pull of the world around them. Their performance lacks any real sense of serving God. And so often in late adolescence they fall away from the Lord.

Is there any more shocking or disillusioning part of Scripture than the reaction of apparently all the other disciples when the ambitious mother of James and John with their full consent came with them to Christ and tried to steal a march on the other disciples, requesting that her sons might sit on Jesus' right hand and left when he established his kingdom (Mt. 20:20-28)? This infuriated the other disciples, and an argument broke out among them as to which of them was the greatest. The Lord Jesus then enunciated the principle of greatness and true leadership in his kingdom: He who would be the top leader should be the servant of all. The greatest would be the one who ministered.

It is unfortunate that the true meaning of the word *minister* has

become obscured in ecclesiastical pomp and ceremony. Today it
signifies a position of respect and prominence, the position of a
leader. The minister of the average church is in an exalted position in relation to his congregation. This is all wrong and contrary
to the meaning of the word *minister,* which is "servant." A small
revolution would take place if we would change the term *minister*
to *servant* and refer to our minister as "Mr. So-and-So, our servant
in the church." But doubtless *servant* would soon accumulate an
aura of dignity, so perhaps this is unimportant. It is the heart attitude worked out in practical life that really counts.

The words of our Lord about true greatness in his kingdom
fell upon deaf ears. As Jesus and the disciples journeyed to Jerusalem, the quarrel between the disciples continued unabated. As
they gathered in the upper room to celebrate the Passover, the
last Passover before Christ would suffer and the occasion when
the Lord instituted the communion, the same strife continued. All
must have been tired from the long walk to Jerusalem. Their san-
daled feet were dusty and dirty and needed washing. There stood a
great pot of water ready, but no servant was present for this normal ablution. One can imagine Christ reclining on a bench and
waiting. Not one of those disciples stepped forward to wash his feet.
Oriental custom and courtesy demanded that the one who commenced washing the feet of the Lord would have to continue and
wash all the disciples' feet. In their present mood, none of them
would stoop to this indignity, and so the Passover meal began.

It was during this meal, according to John 13, that suddenly
and quietly Christ rose from the table, removed his robe and
wrapped a towel around his waist, assuming the role of a slave.
He then took water from the large cistern and began to wash the
disciples' feet. Anyone looking in on that scene would have seen
twelve men reclining around a table littered with a partially completed meal and a slave kneeling before them washing their feet.
And who was that slave? None other than the King of Glory. But

this was in part, in fact, the consummation of the training course in Christian leadership given to these disciples.

While on earth and while training the twelve the Lord Jesus spoke much more about discipleship, about learning to follow him and learning of him, than he ever did about becoming a leader; and, as already mentioned, always his criterion of greatness was servitude. He himself was the perfect servant of Jehovah who lived to do the Father's will.

On my first visit to Jamaica during World War II, not knowing anyone on the island, on Saturday night I asked a bellboy at the hotel if he could direct me to a living church the following morning.

Flashing a smile, he replied, "Sir, I'm a Christian and I'm free tomorrow. Would you care to come with me?"

The next morning he took me to his church, an open Brethren assembly with a congregation that morning of several hundred. The service was good, but largely dominated by missionaries from England.

At the end of the service, a Jamaican elder rose and said that he had been asked to speak on behalf of the church. He addressed the missionaries who mostly were seated together. He thanked them for coming to Jamaica. The Lord had indeed sent them. Had they never come, neither he nor most of the congregation would ever have known Christ. But, he went on to say, the church believed that now their ministry had ended. The church was established with its body of elders, many of whom were now equipped and gifted to lead and to teach and to evangelize in the congregation and the neighborhood.

Naturally, the missionaries had assumed a dominant role in that church. Were they to continue, they would stifle its spiritual growth. The church expressed its love to these missionaries and hoped that some of them would return on occasions from England, perhaps for special ministry of a temporary nature. The spokesman assured them that this decision represented no lack of love or appreciation, no break in fellowship, but was what the congregation believed to be best and to be God's will.

The reaction of those dear pioneer missionaries was interesting but sad. None seemed willing to relinquish a dominant position in that church. Some were in tears; two were indignant. None seemed to understand or remember the example of the apostle Paul, who, in his ministry of church planting, moved from one place to another. As they spoke to me, I expressed surprise at their reaction. I told them that they should be rejoicing, that this was a day of triumph and gladness, a day of victory for them. They had worked themselves out of a job (which, incidentally, has always been the goal of IFES and its staff). The church had been established. They were no longer necessary. But, alas, they had been dominant leaders for so long that they seemed incapable of yielding the reins to others and of stepping down. So often this is the disease of leadership and authority.

It was on this visit that I had my first experience with Jamaica rum. One afternoon I took a long hike several miles beyond the end of the bus route to visit an old Scottish lady missionary to whom I had been introduced the previous Sunday morning. After some refreshment of tea and scones and a time of prayer, I was preparing to take my leave when she said, "Ah, Mr. Woods, and you'll be sure and take home with you a bottle of our good Jamaica rum. I'd never be without it."

Hardly noticing my surprise, she went on, "I take it every night before I go to bed. I used to use rubbing alcohol, but the rum is so much better I bathe and rub my tired feet with it every night."

Christ's great invitation to discipleship is found in Matthew 11:28-29: "Come unto me, all ye that labor and are heavy laden, and I will give you rest. Take my yoke upon you, and learn of me; for I am meek and lowly in heart: and ye shall find rest unto your souls." Christ here is both teacher and example. It is interesting to note that in this verse we have the one allusion that Christ makes about his own personality and character. He says, "I am meek and lowly of heart." This is the Lord of Glory and King of kings. Essentially a disciple is a learner as well as a follower. This blessed servitude to which Christ calls us involves a yoke, but to whom are we to be linked in this way? To none other than Christ himself. What a wonderful partnership! We are to be fellow laborers and servants together with him. The university we attend is the university of life, with Christ as our constant teacher. It is a school of experience from which we never graduate until in heaven we see him face to face. And the essential lesson we learn is a lesson of becoming like Christ, the perfect servant.

The art of learning from Christ and becoming his servant, and so the servant of all men, begins first not in some particular act or service we may do. It begins in our mind, in our attitude toward both ourselves and others. Is there a more profound statement in Scripture than that found in Proverbs 23:7, "For as a man thinketh in his heart, so is he"? What we think, we become. For we are what we think. Hence we should not think of ourselves more highly than we ought to think. It is not easy "to esteem others better than ourselves," but God wants to bring us to the condition where genuinely we have no personal ambition.

Just as Christ found his fulfillment in obeying his Father in heaven so we are to find our self-realization in obeying Christ. To be his servant becomes the place of self-realization and fulfillment, and we desire nothing beyond his will. Here is peace and contentment. We are not working for him, but with him. We are serving him. We are not alone as we pioneer for him, but he goes ahead of us. We are not pushing ahead with our own plans for world evangelism and church growth, but we are following him. We know he has a plan, a blueprint, a timetable. We, his disciples, enjoy just to follow and obey him.

This is no do-nothing philosophy. On the contrary, it will call for a degree of effort, sacrifice and work unimagined. May God bring us to this blessedness of having but one ambition and that to please him. It is as we thus follow the Lord that he makes us effective fishers of men—as we learn of him and become more and more like him, the perfect servant.

As a boy of eleven, I moved with my family to our new home in suburban Sydney, New South Wales. My great desire was for a dog. My parents said nothing as my birthday drew near. Never shall I forget that birthday morning. I was asleep, and Mother and Father came into my room. Mother pulled up the blind, and as I awoke Father quietly put a little furry bundle into the bed. As the eager puppy started to lick my face, I burst into tears of joy and Mother wept with me. Bobs, as he came to be called, became my inseparable companion, at one time meaning more to me than any boyhood friend. So attached did he become that he did not want to go out for a walk unless I were with him. When I studied or read, he was always at my feet. He even seemed to prefer to have me give him his food.

Sometimes my father would call attention to this dog-boy relationship as a picture of what should be the relationship between a Christian servant and his master Christ. God wants us to enter into such a relationship with him wherein we desire to have nothing but what he gives us, to go nowhere but where he directs us, to enjoy his presence and fellowship more than any other association, to have no will but his will. As by his grace we realize and experience such a relationship in which our supreme desire is to please him, then we are becoming great in his eternal kingdom. This, not statistics, is God's standard of spiritual success. By this means he is glorified in us and we are eternally blessed in him.

WINNING PEOPLE TO CHRIST THROUGH PRAYER AND BIBLE STUDY

11

In 1936 I was briefly in New Zealand visiting the various evangelical unions which made up Inter-Varsity in that country. As the result of a long discussion sparked by John Laird of the Scripture Union, a questionnaire was mailed to all of the then existing national evangelical student movements, perhaps seven or eight in number. The question posed was, "What is the single most important activity in your evangelical or Christian union?" The almost unanimous reply—"Our daily prayer meeting." Unfortunately today, because of the changing situation, particularly in nonresidential universities, and the difficulty, in some cases the impossibility, of an entire group of Christians meeting together daily, this practice in some quarters is dying out (although not in Great Britain).

Daily prayer meetings, "DPM's" as they are called, have proved to be the heart throb and central powerhouse for witness to Christ on university campuses. In fact, during the first fifteen years of Inter-Varsity in the U.S.A., the national charter of membership was withheld until a group of students came to realize the necessity of such regular prayer times. Not only were the weekly program of activities and the various needs and problems of chapter members subjects for prayer, but in a very real sense students by prayer were engaged in the spiritual activity of winning their fellow students to Christ. This corporate intercession was supplemented by daily personal prayer during each member's quiet time.

Essentially, true evangelism is a spiritual activity of the Holy Spirit using human instrumentality as his means. If for one moment we allow ourselves to believe it is a human activity, simply aided by the Holy Spirit, we are off base biblically. True it is that we are to go out into all the world heralding the gospel. This is God's means of making Christ known during this age of grace. But the effectiveness of this proclamation depends entirely upon the operation of the Holy Spirit, both upon the one who speaks of Christ and makes the plan of salvation understandable and upon the one who hears. To depend upon the techniques of human persuasion, even though in our earnestness we beseech men to repent and to believe, is to ignore the nature of the new birth.

Psychology and salesmanship may produce decisions which are not the work of God. Martyn Lloyd-Jones in his pamphlet *Conversions: Psychological and Spiritual* points out the very real danger of a so-called conversion which is nothing more than a psychologically induced response and does not represent the regenerating work of the Holy Spirit. He warns against the use of certain methods in mass evangelism which can produce response not necessarily the work of the Holy Spirit. At the same time, he vigorously refutes the contention of anti-Christian psychology that all conversions are nothing more than a psychologically induced response and defends the Holy Spirit's sovereign working, which results in birth from above, or eternal life.

As we pray according to the will of God for our non-Christian friends, often God is preparing us to validate the reality of our faith by a practical demonstration of his love. He enables us to give ourselves to them, which is often a vital part of effective witness. The Holy Spirit prepares us to speak to them in his power and prompts us as we speak. He works, too, in the one who is the object of our prayer and witness, enabling him to listen, to understand and to consider honestly the claims of Christ and Christ's offer of forgiveness and salvation.

To attempt to win anyone to Christ apart from urgent intercessory prayer is to fail to understand the condition of the lost. An unsaved person has been deliberately blinded by Satan to prevent any natural possibility of his coming to spiritual sight and receiving Christ (2 Cor. 4:3-4). He has an appalling absence of personal concern, stemming from the fact that spiritually he is dead. An unconverted person in and of himself is totally incapable of turning to Christ.

A ministry of intercession for the lost, particularly those the Holy Spirit lays upon our hearts, is a God-given responsibility. Christians are a body of priests interceding to God. "All evangelism must begin with prayer and no human service and/or desire can take the place of intercession," says Lewis Sperry Chafer in *True Evangelism*, a book unsurpassed in its teaching about biblical evangelism (p. 88). This in no way lessens the necessity of teaching, preaching and pleading with people to come to Christ, but by such intercessory prayer the Holy Spirit is released to "plow up the fallow ground" and to prepare men and women for the message of the gospel.

Chafer goes on to state,

It is the teaching of Scripture that the action of the mighty power of God in convicting and illuminating the unsaved is in large measure dependent upon the priestly intercession of the believer. . . . Where believing prayer has been offered with expectation toward God alone there has always been evidence of the power of God unto salvation according to his covenant of promises. Fundamentally, the personal element in true soulwinning work is more a service of pleading FOR souls than a service of pleading WITH souls. (*True Evangelism*, pp. 91 and 93)

Usually, although not always, true conversion is a process that ends in a crisis. Part of this necessary process is the sowing of the seed of the Word of God, usually through a study of the Scriptures. There is a great deal of evidence within the member movements of the International Fellowship of Evangelical Students that more university students have been truly converted through Bible study than through any other means. This should not surprise us. Where does one reap a harvest of fruit, vegetables or grain where there has been no sowing? As in earthly endeavor, so it is with the spiritual. Repeatedly Scripture uses natural law to illustrate the spiritual realm. The good seed of the Word must be sown. It must be watered and nourished by the Holy Spirit, and in due course it yields the harvest.

In previous generations, this seed was sown in the hearts of boys and girls in their homes as Christian parents instructed and trained their children in the ways of God. Later, in church and Sunday school, more seed was sown, perhaps to lie dormant for a long period. Later it sprang into life. Since the 1950s we increasingly face a new situation. There is a growing majority of young people who are biblically illiterate. They simply have not been taught. The seed has not been sown. For many, this ignorance may be compared with that of some tribe which has never heard of Christ. Today most university students are almost as ignorant of the truth of the gospel as some primitive aborigines. Many are in a worse condition in that, rejecting the little knowledge they have, they have renounced the Christian faith outright.

Among primitives, a missionary must teach the Word. Months of this sowing may be needed before there is any response and harvest. To reach students today, therefore, two things are needed in addition to necessary prayer: The gospel must be taught and the reality of its message must be authenticated in the life of Christian students who are seeking to influence their fellow students for Christ. Principally this validation must be expressed in practical love and concern coupled with a living demonstration of Christian ethics and morality. Failure to demonstrate the love of God and the absence of a lifestyle which represents biblical values and standards create the impression that the Christian faith is "an old wives' tale" devoid of any real content and significance. Herein lies a great failure of the church. Unless life in Christ is demonstrated in this mechanistic world as a live option and an alternative to secularism and materialism, unless we can demonstrate a coherent world and life view which is consistent and self-validating in its practical application in daily life, then it is hard to imagine any great Christian impact upon this generation.

Such a life also can only be lived by daily dependence upon the Holy Spirit and his power. The entire Christian enterprise is a divine-human endeavor with God taking the initiative and providing the enablement, and with the Christian, God's child, being his yielded, living instrument used to accomplish his eternal purpose.

Some years ago I was invited to preach the "going down" sermon at the end of term at Oxford University for the Oxford Intercollegiate Christian Union (Inter-Varsity). More than five hundred were present at that service, which in a sense was the climax to the OICCU's witness during the preceding weeks. In a very happy way that evening, I felt that I was little more than background music. My concern was that I should not create any discord. Christian students had not simply given their friends an invitation to this service; they had *brought* them. During term they had shown these unbelieving men and women friendship. They had tried to live before them as Christians. They had brought them each week to dormitory or residence hall Bible studies.

That night was a time of reaping. In the sermon I endeavored to make clear the gospel and urged commitment to Christ. There was no public appeal. At the conclusion of the service, as many were quietly leaving, all over that auditorium Christians with open Bible were pointing their friends to Christ. Quite a number were converted that night, but this was no sudden harvest. The seed of God's Word had been sown faithfully. Christ had lived out his life through many of those Christian students. The converts of that evening were the natural, supernatural outworking of an academic term of effective witness to Christ.

This same approach is used in home Bible classes where Christian women invite their friends in the neighborhood not just to a coffee klatch but to study the Scriptures. Perhaps eternity will reveal that truer and more fruitful evangelism is being carried out by this quiet, unostentatious approach than is accomplished by the enormous spectaculars which are held at such fantastic cost, which attract so much attention and yet which sometimes result in little more than empty clamor and frenetic activity.

Such Bible study groups are often called *evangelistic Bible studies*. This label seems to me too stylized, too pointed, and, if known to the unconverted, is apt to turn him off. Better far simply to study the Scriptures in faith and dependence upon the Holy Spirit, leaving him to work his work. This does not mean that we fail to urge commitment to Christ. The great danger of group study is that it will be allowed to degenerate into fruitless speculation where personal reaction—"It seems to me" or "I think"—becomes the authority rather than Scripture itself.

In the 1930s I conducted a study group at the University of Toronto. We called it "Life or Merely Pretense." Each meeting began with a simple Bible reading, or exposition. This was followed by a no-holds-barred session in which any question or objection could be voiced. But the Bible always was accepted as our final court of appeal. Numbers grew from a handful to well over one hundred.

This leads me to comment on the almost lost art of biblical exposition and the function of the Bible teacher who authoritatively expounds the Word of God. Today many Christians prefer to discuss, which is often a sharing of ignorance and prejudice rather than a humble willingness to listen and to learn.

What are the elements in true expository preaching, whether the exposition of a phrase, a verse or a longer passage? The first task of the expositor is *exegesis,* which means to arrive at the true meaning of the words used, their relationship to one another and the essential message the writer was passing on. Once this message is understood, it is the task of the expositor to extract the essential biblical principles which lie behind what the writer is saying. Until we understand the principles involved, we are hardly in a position to move on to particulars and application.

When it comes to application, the expositor must understand the context in which the passage was written, and then whether the author intended his message to be applied personally and practically or figuratively. If in those days a personal, practical application was being called for, we may rightly suppose that a similar application will obtain in our day. He must then make the transfer to our generation and our present life situation and help us understand the modern application. He must bring the truth down to where we live.

Another essential element in all true exposition is that the expositor must call for a verdict. One of the troubles with straight Bible teaching is that it can degenerate into an intellectual exercise, into the mere culling and receiving of information. But the Bible is always more than information. It is God's Word, the expression of God's will. And, consequently, verdict or decision is demanded. Personal response to the Word of God is of the highest and most essential importance in all biblical exposition and often is the key to expository preaching which brings about true conversion. Solid expository preaching can and should be an essential part of the evangelistic undertaking.

Quiet, steady, continuous evangelism involving intercessory prayer and the study and preaching of the Scriptures is not a task for a selected, gifted few. It is not limited to the minister of the church and his ordained assistants. Rather, it is the privilege and responsibility of every Christian. Regardless of special gifts, all are called and commissioned to this task. Every Christian is a missionary sent by God, a witness to Jesus Christ, in his or her way a herald of the gospel. God's supreme method is men—men and women indwelt and filled with the Holy Spirit. Can the Holy Spirit infill a technique or a formula which is mechanically applied? I doubt it.

One danger we face is that in our eagerness to see our friends become Christians we romanticize the gospel. We present it as a wonderful plan for his life, with only some shades or overtones of eternity. I have heard it suggested that if we come to Christ a happy and wonderful life is ours—a great job, a beautiful girl, a wonderful family, even affluence (for affluence is equated with God's blessing). The word of the apostle Paul in Philippians 1:29, "It is given in the behalf of Christ, not only to believe on him, but also to suffer for his sake," is hardly if ever mentioned.

Further, we must be careful to emphasize that the Lord Jesus is the Savior from sin. He was given the name *Jesus* because he would save his people from their sin. The essential reason for his coming into this world was to deal with the problem of sin—both cosmic sin and personal sin. "He came to put away sin by the sacrifice of himself" (Heb. 9:26). If therefore a person has no desire to be saved from sin and its penalty, Christ has nothing whatsoever to offer him, nothing to say to him. All the multitudinous blessings God longs to pour upon his children are conditioned upon their settling this matter of their transgression on the basis of the substitutionary atonement accomplished by Christ on the cross.

We must also understand the threefold aspect of salvation. Not only does Christ save us from the guilt and penalty of sins committed in the past; he also provides forgiveness and cleansing for sins we commit day by day as we confess these trespasses to Christ our great High Priest on the basis of the efficacy of the blood of Christ. Salvation in the life of one who has believed is to be effective in delivering him from the ruling power of sin in daily life. Nowhere does the Bible suggest that once we are saved, we are free to live as we please. Paul cries out in horror at such a thought: "Shall we continue in sin, that grace may abound? God forbid (Rom. 6:1-2). So true conversion involves taking sides with God against sin, and longing and trusting for deliverance from the domination of sin (which by no means suggests sinless perfection). Finally, we have the prospect and promise of our final deliverance from a sinful environment, from the presence of sin and from our old nature, which so avidly responds and acquiesces to temptation. All of this is involved in salvation from sin, which is the essence of God's deliverance. These three elements of salvation need to be emphasized in all evangelism, whether in interceding for those who are lost or in opening up the Word of God or in actually proclaiming the gospel and leading people to commitment to the Lord Jesus.

Having written all this and insisted that there is a normal, biblical way God deals with men and women to bring about their salvation, I must also emphasize that the sovereign God is not bound. He is not limited to any particular approach or method. Frequently one hears of miraculous exceptions. When facing an impending crisis or some perilous situation, a man may cry out to the Lord and his conversion be divinely effected. On occasion, God breaks in upon a person. Sometimes in a secular situation. Sometimes with the person's having little or no real understanding of the gospel. In a theater. In a foxhole.

We do not, however, base our evangelism upon the exceptional activities of the Holy Spirit, but rather upon the spiritual laws of

God, his ways of working with men as described in the Bible. God's work must be done in God's way and at God's time. Consequently, method and timing must be biblical and in accord with the workings of the Holy Spirit. Thus God is glorified in the process of our evangelism, in the manner in which the gospel is presented and in the mighty working of the Holy Spirit, as he and he alone calls men and women from spiritual death and blindness to life and light in Jesus Christ.

MAN'S NEED, GOD'S GLORY

12

As a boy, at more than one missionary convention I listened to an emotional piece of imagination that carried a tremendous wallop. It went something like this:

A scene in heaven—Christ is risen and seated at the right hand of the Father. Angels approach him with the question, "Lord, on earth you have fulfilled all righteousness, you have manifested the Father, you have demonstrated your deity in the face of unbelief. On the cross you put away sin, you defeated Satan, you won forgiveness of sins and the possibility of salvation for all mankind. Now every man and woman has the opportunity of eternal salvation. Will you return to earth to proclaim this good news?"

"No!"

"Will you then send us to be your evangelists?"

"No!"

"Well then, please tell us your plan."

"I have left eleven disciples on earth and there is Paul. They and all who follow them are my ambassadors."

"And what if they fail?"

"I have no other plan!"

Then followed the challenge and call not to fail Christ: The salvation of mankind is at stake. It depends upon us. Who will go? It was a moving, stirring appeal—but unscriptural.

Then there is that old missionary chestnut where man's need becomes God's call: Fifteen husky men are lifting up one end of a huge and heavy log; one emaciated fellow struggles in vain to lift the other. This supposedly is a picture of the Christian strength in the Western world as compared with the truly desperate need and paucity of Christian workers in other parts of the world. The inference is obvious. At least half a dozen of those brawny fellows at the one end of the log should volunteer to go to the aid of their isolated brother. And so the need becomes God's call to world evangelism and missionary endeavor. This also is unscriptural.

Today, particularly in North America but unfortunately spreading to many parts of the world, we see an emphasis upon results and success as the criteria of God's approval. The person with many conversion scalps hanging from his wigwam is the one God is blessing. Multiple professions of conversion are the accepted sign of God's approval and expected heavenly reward. Method and technique are hailed and conscripted as the key to the completion of the task of world evangelism and a final ingathering of unimagined multitudes to Christ's kingdom before his return. New methods and techniques of Church Growth lead to the conversion of whole tribes and communities. Amazing success stories abound on every hand. We are told that today there are stereotyped methods of presenting Christ which virtually guarantee conversion. There are new insights and approaches which enable us to communicate, convince and almost convert thousands, and so this modern nostrum goes on.

The difficulty with these new approaches is that they are not completely false; they contain elements of biblical truth. Every believer has a God-given responsibility to witness and to evangelize. The disparity between evangelicals in the Western world on one hand and in the communist world and the third and fourth worlds on the other may well be used by the Holy Spirit in calling us to missionary service and world evangelism. Pentecost demonstrates the importance of communication and the need for a degree of cultural identification in missionary endeavor. The problem is that these elements in Christian service worldwide are all too obvious, but they are only a small part of the truth, perhaps a much smaller part than we suppose. And a half-truth in and of itself is an untruth.

Some time ago in South America a conference was held on Evangelism and Church Growth. Novel techniques were propounded. Finally a friend of mine asked a Church Growth enthusiast, "What is your biblical basis for these theories?" The extraordinary reply from this well-known evangelical seminary leader, "We haven't got one yet, but we have a new professor at _____. He will develop this for us."

All heresy and error begins when we start with man rather than with God and his inerrant revelation of his truth and will inscripturated in the Bible. Heresy in the Christian church is a mixture of truth and non-truth. It is mostly a tale of those who in some way or other turn from God and his revealed Word—from rational revelation—to man and irrationalism. When we put man and his need before God and his glory, we have begun our descent into the abyss.

Years ago at a banquet in Washington, D. C., a certain senator from Virginia introduced the main speaker, Billy Graham, and compared him to Jesus Christ. As I sat there, I became almost ill with apprehension until Billy rose to speak. Courteously but firmly he utterly repudiated the words of the chairman, saying, "God will never share his glory with any man."

Christ came to glorify God. He did this first by living a perfect life of obedience to his Father, living only to do the Father's will.

God the Father on more than one occasion broke the silence of heaven and said, "My beloved Son in whom I am well pleased. My beloved Son, hear him."

In his earthly ministry Christ also destroyed the works of the devil and cast out Satan, the god of this world, who on account of Adam and Eve's sin was able to usurp God's authority on earth and become its ruler. If the glory of God was the supreme goal of God the Son on earth and on the cross and in his resurrection—and it was—how much more should it be the compelling motivation and primary objective for us, Christ's disciples!

But, we may say, if by a new technique and method we can greatly multiply Christian converts, is this not to Christ's glory? First of all, we can never convert anyone. "Salvation is of the Lord." Then our ability to glorify God can never be in our own strength and in our own initiative but only under the leading and enablement of the Holy Spirit, who alone guides and speaks according to the written Word of God. The supreme work of the Holy Spirit during this age of grace is not even his work in us believers but rather his effort to glorify Christ the Lord (Jn. 16:13-14). This in part takes place as the Holy Spirit becomes our teacher, our guide, our enabler; as he helps us in relation to God's will. But always our service must be with a view to the glory of God.

It must be recognized that God's work must be done in God's way if it is to be to God's glory. If our ministry draws attention to ourselves, our cleverness, our inventiveness, our technique, our method, it may easily fail to glorify God. A careful study of 1 Corinthians 1:18—2:16 makes this abundantly clear.

Salvation is the result of God's powerful working. God's power is demonstrated by the absurdity, naturally considered, of preaching Christ crucified. The salvation of any man is dependent upon God's sovereign call.

God upsets and rejects the wisdom and technique of man; he confounds the wise and the mighty by taking the weak, the despised and the ignorant, those who are nothing, and by demonstrating in them his salvation to his glory. God will eventually destroy the wisdom and understanding of this world. And so the brilliant scholar Paul humbles himself by writing, "I am determined to know nothing among you save Christ and him crucified" (1 Cor. 2:2). As believers we have not received the spirit of this world but the Spirit which is of God.

Therefore, to teach psychological techniques and human persuaders, to adopt the worldly methods of advertising and propaganda, to employ methods of mass media and movement, to follow these God-rejected techniques and then to claim that the results are of God would seem to me (to say the least) questionable. To study the history of the evangelical effort in Japan in the 1950s under the benevolence of the late, great General MacArthur and to examine what happened or did not happen to the hundreds of thousands who were reported to have received Christ during those frenzied days is an illustration of man's work to man's glory in contrast to God's work to God's glory. (This is not to say that some of those among the many thousands who raised their hands were not regenerated.)

Man, even converted man, with his continuing egoism and sinful nature is incessantly proud and independent. Naturally we hate to receive authoritative instruction, to take orders. We want our own way. How difficult it is for a person to bend his will to God's will, to bend his mind to God's mind. It is this drive to be independent, to make our own plans, to work out our own life and our own salvation apart from God that is our downfall.

Why is it so difficult for us to become little children dependent and obedient upon our heavenly Father? God has given us his blueprint and program for us, for this world, for world evangelism and for the future. He has told us what he wants done and how he wants it done. But we prefer to make our own plans and program.

This "do-it-yourself" philosophy dominates us. We are glad for

God's occasional assistance when we ask him. We are happy to present to him the success of our own efforts. So often he has to reject this. We are busy working for him, trying to do what he has not asked us to do, working in a way he cannot accept. How much wood, hay and stubble is there in our lives and Christian service? God help us to abandon totally our independence and to submit totally to his will and his word, to be willing to be nothing, to be nobody, in order that he may be glorified. God help us to reject the damnable philosophy of success and results so current in evangelical circles today. God help us to reject the false dictum that if a thing works, if it succeeds and has great results, then it must be of God. *God is not a pragmatist.*

When we speak of God's blueprint, we mean of course a blueprint in principle not in detail. The details are made plain by the illumination of the Holy Spirit guiding through the Word of God, as I have explained more fully in chapter 4.

No, God has not abandoned his work on earth to us. Christ will fulfill his promise, "I will build my church" (Mt. 16:18). He is the master-builder and we his obedient workers have the privilege of being laborers together with him. It is not always clear to us what he is doing. We are not always certain how the details in which we are engaged really fit into his master-plan. But we continue in faith, often serving and working for him in obscurity and in a measure of darkness, "unhonored and unsung." But there is a coming day when the prize for faithfulness and obedience will be awarded and we shall hear him, our risen and glorified Lord, say to us, "Well done, good and faithful servant. Enter into the joy of your Lord."

If we are to serve God acceptably, his glory must become our consuming ambition. To live and to serve him in order that he may be glorified must take precedence over every other consideration and consequence in every aspect of the Christian ministry.

CALLED TO
BE DIFFERENT

13

"**In our organization we have campus beauty queens,** star athletes, top men on campus, genuine youth leaders —nothing but the best for Christ."

"Tonight on our platform we have a successful millionaire, a converted model and a fashion leader from Europe's Jet Set. For our opening speaker we have the glamorous, atheist Secretary of State—and Senator So-and-So will introduce him." But isn't he a Mormon official? "Yes, maybe he is, but he is important. You see we must attract the attention of the world's press if we are to succeed for Christ."

The apostle Paul is opening his campaign in Rome and has invited Emperor Nero to give the welcoming address, and Claudia, a recently converted courtesan, who has a glorious voice and is world famous, will sing her number "My Eye Is on the Eagle."

The apostle Paul arrived in Rome a disgraced Roman citizen in chains, a prisoner in bonds for the Lord Jesus Christ. He had previously written to the little church in Rome, "I am eager to preach the gospel to you also who are in Rome" (Rom. 1:15, RSV). His official welcome was a prison. But he was faithful to his Lord. From the prison he wrote to his brothers and sisters in Philippi, "It has been granted to you that for the sake of Christ you should not only believe in him but also suffer for his sake" (Phil. 1:29, RSV).

Some time ago I read the staff manual of a great international organization. Every detail was carefully prescribed—perfume, deodorant, shortness of mini-skirt, hairstyle, lipstick, rouge, eye shadow, ad nauseam. "But you see our staff must present the image of the fashionable, successful American young man and woman in Christ. We must be attractive if we are to attract people to Christ."

Paul wrote, "Don't let the world around squeeze you into its own mold" (Rom. 12:1 Phillips).

Obviously the opposite of what we are caricaturing here is also untrue. Nowhere does Scripture suggest we must trail around in antediluvian weeds, looking like the ghost of Christmas past, in order to be an effective witness. But is the present-day emphasis upon glamorous externality in evangelism scriptural? Does God's blessing depend upon public relations, the successful image, famous people and computerized predictions of results? Or does it depend upon faithfulness to the Word of God, which includes faithfulness to the *way* God wants things done as well as a concern for the ends themselves? God's work must be done in God's way and at God's time, for it represents God's will.

What relationship is there between an appeal to current fashion, dress, hairstyle and make-up and the call of the gospel to repentance toward God and faith in Jesus Christ? Some years ago I was a guest in the home of a well-to-do fundamentalist minister, noted for his sartorial splendor. As we left for church that Sunday morning, he was dressed in another new suit, shirt and tie. Smiling he said to me, "We must adorn the gospel of our Lord Jesus Christ, you know. Ha! Ha!" Christ, however, taught that the evidence to the world that ours is a valid Christian faith will be our love to one another within the Christian brotherhood. New Testament references to dress emphasize modesty, for example, a hairstyle that is unostentatious, unelaborate, simple. Surely the thrust of the New Testament is that the believer is to be inconspicuous—neither a fashion leader nor so far out of step that he draws attention to himself. It is the task of a Christian witness to draw attention to Christ, not to himself.

Has modern evangelicalism in the Western world missed God's way? Are we guilty of misinterpreting Scripture? Have we fallen into the error of believing that a spiritual ministry affecting one's eternal welfare can be aided and abetted by natural, physical, material, fleshly means?

Our Lord prayed, "The world has hated them, because they are not of the world, even as I am not of the world" (Jn. 17:14). But aren't we courting the world by these approaches? Aren't we asking the world to patronize the gospel? Have we forgotten the warning that the world which hated, rejected and crucified Christ will also reject us, if we are really faithful to him? Are we seeking the acceptance of this world rather than the acceptance of God?

In the last century there was a gifted Old Testament scholar who also was a devout Christian and Bible expositor. He was invited to take a chair of Old Testament at Oxford University, so he went to discuss this possibility with the university authorities. They told him that were he to accept this position it would give him standing and recognition. They ended with an appeal that he accept this post, for it would give him acceptance in the world. His quiet answer was, "Which world, gentlemen?" and he declined the position.

Such a response may seem extreme; yet it contains a germ of truth that perhaps we have forgotten today.

Our Lord in his high-priestly prayer said that we who belong to him are not to be of this world, characterized by this world, poured into the mold of this world, even as the Lord Jesus was not. But the direction of much modern evangelical activity appears to seek acceptance by the world, which crucified Jesus Christ.

Christ prayed that we might remain in this world to be its light and salt, but he never told us to be conformed to its pattern or to seek its approval—in order to gain acceptance for the gospel. Never should we seek to obliterate the difference between Christians and non-Christians. Too often I have heard a gospel appeal something like this, "You don't have to give up anything to be a Christian. All you have to do is move in with Jesus Christ. He will bless you. He will help you and guide you regarding your career. He will work out your marriage. You have the assurance of a beautiful and successful life if you move in with Jesus Christ."

This is a lie from hell. You have to give up everything to be a Christian: You have to give yourself to the Lord. Nowhere does the Bible promise a Christian "health, wealth and the pursuit of happiness," but rather sacrifice, suffering, perhaps even death.

The apostle Paul under the inspiration of the Holy Spirit made it quite clear that those who desire to live a godly life in Christ Jesus will be persecuted in this world (2 Tim. 3:13). Persecution takes many forms. In the academic world, for instance, to have your ideas rejected and to be judged narrow-minded and obscurantist is persecution.

Our failure to emphasize the radical and essential difference between a Christian and a non-Christian, between the Christian way of life and the non-Christian way of life, is a root cause of today's weakness and spiritual ineffectiveness. If the world ignores Christians and ignores the church, it is because we fawn before the world, seek its favors and delicacies, and strive to imitate its ways.

The Bible makes the difference between a Christian and a non-Christian unmistakably clear: "If any man be in Christ, he is a new creature [or new creation]: old things are passed away; behold, all things are become new" (2 Cor. 5:17). "No man can serve two masters. You cannot serve God and mammon [or the world]" (Mt. 6:24). This difference is not primarily an external difference, although inevitably it will express itself in outward behavior and appearance. It is essentially an inner difference.

A true Christian has a new and different mind set from a non-Christian. He views himself and everything around him from a different perspective. His value judgments are different; his goals are different; the orientation of his life is different; his reactions are different. He is no longer limited by the temporal and physical space-time existence of earth; he has eternity in his heart; he is a pilgrim. Earth is not his true and ultimate home.

As a consequence, a Christian's responses, reactions and attitudes to the world around him and its happenings are radically different from those of an unconverted person. A Christian knows he is God's child. God's hand is upon him, guiding him, protecting him, providing for him and urging him forward toward heaven. He has an inner sense of security and, consequently, God's peace. No truer word has been spoken than that in Proverbs 23:7, "For as a man thinketh in his heart, so is he." Because a Christian thinks differently, he is a different person. He believes in eternal values, which far out-distance material and temporal concerns. He knows that if he is putting Christ's cause and kingdom foremost in his thinking and living, God has promised to provide the three basic necessities of physical existence—food, clothing and shelter. He believes God when God says, "I will provide sufficient food for your physical need. I will give you enough clothing. I will provide adequate shelter." God never promises luxury or affluence but only that which is sufficient, although in his grace he usually supplies far and above the level of mere subsistence.

Not only is a Christian radically different from a non-Christian in the way he thinks and reacts, but he is different in his associations with other people. Some are his brothers and sisters in Christ for whom he has a special bond and responsibility and intimacy, something that is utterly incapable of realization by the unconverted. The Christian brotherhood, which binds believers together by Christ's law of love, supersedes every fraternal association the world has ever conceived. True, people may have deep friendships on a purely human level, but unless both partners are in Christ the dimension of eternity is completely unachievable. A Christian also must love those outside of Christ—he must love his neighbors as himself—but until they are in Christ he can never have the same intimate bond with them that exists between believers.

Nowhere is this clearer than in the marriage union. There are few greater sins than for a Christian deliberately and knowingly to marry a non-Christian. This Christian is condemning his or her unborn children to an unconverted father or mother whose natural tendency will inevitably be to draw them away from Jesus Christ, no matter how amiable the marriage bond on a human level may be. Under this unequal yoke, husband and wife can never pray together. They are incapable of sharing the deepest issues of life. One is bound for heaven, the other for hell. When these issues are realized, such a union can be little less than hell on earth, if the Christian is really thinking and living as a true follower of Jesus Christ.

If we have this Christian mind, the possibility of marrying a non-Christian is inconceivable. Dare I curse my unborn child with a mother or a father who is essentially a child of Satan? Dare I jeopardize the eternal future of my unborn children by a parent who is alien to God? Dare I marry a person who is incapable of praying with me and praying with my children and teaching them the truth of God? Can there possibly be any union and communion between a man and woman who, though legally and physically united, yet are not one in Christ Jesus?

In a marriage union where there is an unequal yoke we can see most clearly the essential difference between a Christian and a non-Christian. But why can't we perceive this same difference in every other binding relationship?

We must bear in mind the false extremes to which some have gone—an employee saying, for instance, that he cannot work for an employer who is a non-Christian. This is not an unequal yoke. On the other hand, a business partnership between a Christian and non-Christian can easily lead to spiritual disaster, or at least sinful compromise.

It is of tremendous importance that we realize what takes place when we are born again. The new birth is no humanistic decision for Christ. When by the enablement of the Holy Spirit we commit ourselves body, soul and spirit to the Lord Jesus, by that same Holy Spirit we are baptized into the body of Christ, we are born children of God, the divine nature is imparted and implanted in us. The Holy Spirit makes our heart his dwelling place; we become radically different in a spiritual sense, though physically we may be the same person.

What God has effected in us spiritually is then to be expressed outwardly in our daily life. It commences with the mind; and the renewed mind is of essential importance, for it determines our behavior pattern, our sense of values, the character of our relationships, in fact the totality of our life on earth among men and women. It is the basis and means of the transformation of which Paul speaks in Romans 12:1-2, whereby God gives us an eternal perspective, a Christian orientation, an entirely new thrust and direction to our thinking. Unless we have begun to think as a Christian, unless we have a Christian biblical mind, we cannot possibly behave as God would have us act in this world. Not until the new birth takes place is the essential difference that God expects and requires made possible; only then can it be put into effect day by day in our association with others.

THE QUEST FOR IDENTITY AND SELF-ACCEPTANCE

14

Who am I? Why was I born? Am I anybody anyway?

I was not free to choose my parents, the color of my skin or my race. I did not determine my intelligence quotient, my personality, my natural disposition or my appearance. I had no say in my charm, or lack of it.

What about my natural talents and abilities? Was I born with such physical coordination that I could become an athlete? Did I inherit histrionic ability so that I could become a success on the stage? Was I free to choose whether I could become a scholar, a musician, a great painter, a successful businessman or a teacher? Even whether I am an extrovert or an introvert to a large extent was determined by my heredity over which I had no control.

Furthermore, I was not free to choose my primary environment —the part of the world where I was born, its climate, its culture, its educational and economic possibilities, its public health, its liability to disease.

And now I am still surrounded by all sorts of uncontrollable factors and hazards—a national economy, prosperity or depression, unemployment, war, peace, accident, natural disaster, epidemic.

The only possible conclusion, when I see myself shaped by so many factors beyond my control, is that there is no such thing as freedom in an absolute sense.

Yet...I...am...I.

We live in a highly competitive society. In spite of any kind of political idealism the facts of life force us to the conclusion that in this world the only right that really counts is the right of the strongest—"Right is might." Human society is essentially selfish, lacking in compassion. It is cruel, indifferent to the needs of others, individualistic, ruthless and competitive. Its great driving motivations are self-preservation and self-aggrandizement. Despite a veneer of civilization our society is really a society of fang and claw. It is dishonest, immoral, callous, bestial and only occasionally altruistic. The Bible describes human society as a collection of rebels against God, contaminated and corrupted by sin, ruled by Satan the god of this world.

When Satan tempted the Lord Jesus, at one stage he offered him all the kingdoms of this world if Christ would only worship him. Never once did Christ dispute Satan's right and prerogative to offer this. It was soon after God had given to Adam and Eve, our first parents, the dominion over this world that they forfeited it by submitting themselves to the will and temptation of Satan, who upon their submission to him immediately became the god of this world, its ruler and the one who has dominion over it; and man himself became Satan's slave.

If I accept the Bible's verdict about me, and if I am honest enough to know myself, I am a rebel, a sinner, naturally refusing God and God's government, dominated by self-indulgence and self-preservation.

When I became a true Christian, I committed myself to the law

and will of Jesus Christ, but I continued to be myself with the sum
total of all my natural assets and liabilities. I am what I am by
heredity. I am what I am by environment. Now that I am a Christian, people around me are no different, even though I may view
them differently through the eyes of a child of God. Many will have
a pleasant facade; most will be inwardly selfish. It is in this world
of fang and claw that I must know myself, accept myself and live
for Christ and his kingdom.

One of the most wonderful things about our relationship
with God is that he accepts us just as we are. He does not set up
some standard to which we must attain before he will receive us.
He knows us far better than we can ever know ourselves, and
knowing and seeing us just as we are he accepts us. But more than
that, he loves us just as we are. There are no truer words than those
in the fourth verse of that familiar, almost hackneyed, evangelistic
hymn, "Just as I Am." Unfortunately, this hymn has become the
standard appeal at the end of the average evangelistic meeting,
but more properly it is a hymn to be sung upon the knees of our
hearts at the communion table:

Just as I am, Thou wilt receive,
Wilt welcome, pardon, cleanse, relieve;
Because Thy promise I believe,
O Lamb of God, I come.

If God accepts me just as I am, and receives me just as I am, is it
impossible for me to accept myself?

God's love for me, his acceptance of me, is never determined by
my performance. If I as a Christian live a life of separation from
the world and victory over sin, a life filled with the Holy Spirit,
does this mean that God loves me more than he loves other Christians who are not living a spiritual life? If I bring honor and glory
to the name of the Lord Jesus and do not live as a prodigal Christian, does this mean that I merit more of God's love? God could
never love you and me more than he did when we were yet in a

state of sin, enmity, alienation, refusal and rebellion against him. For then he gave his only Son to die for us. This is the measure of God's love for us.

I shall never forget one of the last conversations I had with my father before I left Australia for North America. I was twenty, soon to turn twenty-one. My father said something like this to me, "Stacey, you are my son, this is your home, and I love you. I hope and pray that you will follow the way of God and that I may be proud of you. But, if things should turn otherwise and you should fall into sin, even disgrace, always remember I am your father. I will always love you as my son, and no matter what may happen this home is always your home and you can be sure of a welcome. You can be sure that you will always be received and loved."

How I thank God for my father, from whom I first learned the elementary understanding of the love of my heavenly Father. How I thank God that I knew I was accepted just as I was and that love was not doled out so much love for so much good behavior.

God loves us simply because he loves us, not because there is anything good in us, not because we merit his love. This is not only true for us as individuals, it was also strangely true of the nation Israel. "The Lord did not set his love upon you, nor choose you, because you were more in number than any people, for you were the fewest of all people: but because the LORD loved you" (Deut. 7:7-8).

If therefore God accepts me and loves me just as I am, if his love for me is in no way determined by my performance, why is it then not possible for me to accept myself as I am? To be accepted by God, to be received by him as a member of his family, to be adopted by him as one of his sons and heirs, is the greatest acceptance conceivable. In the light of all this, for me to refuse to accept myself as I am, with the sum total of all the assets and liabilities which God has given me, is really to dishonor God, even to refuse him.

Too often children come to feel and to believe that their parents' love for them is determined by their performance. A boy is led to believe that if he dresses properly and keeps himself clean, is obedient and does well at school, his parents will love him more than if he were careless, irresponsible and a failure. A girl may come to believe that her parents' love for her depends upon her behavior and attitude toward them, her success at school and the way she conforms to the family pattern. When this is the case, love becomes a matter of quid pro quo—so much love for so much obedience and conformity. Such an attitude is a total denial of the God-intended family relationship.

Too often parents try to bend their children and subject their children's personality to a parental concept of an acceptable but rigid way of life. They insist that their children conform to a certain family lifestyle, dress, behavior. And if a child expresses individuality and a personality independent of the parents, this creates such strain and tension that sometimes the child feels rejected and is forced to leave home in order to be himself. This is not to say that there should be no family lifestyle, but it should never be so absolute and unrelenting that it is incapable of adjustment. If a parent's love is dependent upon the performance and behavior of his children, this is no longer love. What should have been love has degenerated into a commercial contract. Naturally, parents are proud of their children and find satisfaction in them when they perform acceptably, but this is something altogether different from the love-bond which is the essential relationship between mother and father and son and daughter.

God loves you and me as much as he loves anybody else. This is not to ignore or to deny that some Christians bring honor and glory to God, while others bring shame to his name, that some will receive reward while others will be saved "so as by fire," in other words, by the skin of their teeth. But this is different from God's love and his acceptance of us on the merit of the Substitute who died for us, the Lord Jesus Christ.

Even though there may exist what the Bible describes as temporary and transitory differences between individuals—race, ability, color of skin, intelligence, level of affluence, opportunity—this is not the end of the story. This is not all of life. Is there a more joyful, thrilling and exciting truth in Scripture than the truth of our predestination? God has chosen us in Christ from before the foundation of the world, and the purpose of his choice and the destiny he has predetermined for us is to make us completely like Jesus Christ.

When the Lord Jesus was on earth, God on more than one occasion broke the silence of heaven to say, "This is my beloved Son, in whom I am well pleased: hear him." God was so thoroughly satisfied and delighted with his Son, the man Christ Jesus, God incarnate, the last Adam, that he decided to populate Heaven with people just like him. This is the goal of our sanctification, which began when we were born again and baptized into the body of Christ. From that moment on, the Holy Spirit has worked in us to make us inwardly and outwardly like the Lord Jesus.

When we see him, that work will be completed. Differences between one another really will be obliterated, for we shall all be like the Lord Jesus, although retaining our own personality and identity. As a consequence, natural differences between us in this life, many of which are peripheral and incidental, are of no eternal significance.

But there is something more. Psychologists tell us that usually the difference between success and failure is not so much caused by intelligence, personality or appearance, but rather by motivation. Many are millionaires in terms of natural ability, talent, opportunity and possibility, but they never amount to anything. They are failures, even in this life. Whereas many others of mediocre ability and limited opportunity become tremendous successes. Why is this? The reason is motivation.

God is the great motivator. And the miracle of the working of the Holy Spirit in Christians is the way in which he takes the most ordinary individuals with the most limited abilities and opportunities and motivates them to perform to their optimum. So people who naturally would have amounted to very little left on their own become outstanding leaders. They rise far above their fellows. Like Christ's feeding the five thousand when he took a boy's lunch, five barley rolls and a couple of pickled or dried fish, and fed a multitude, Christ can take you and me, very limited and circumscribed though we may be, and can—I dare to say *will*—use us to a degree far beyond any natural expectation.

Think of an automobile capable of traveling 100 miles an hour, idling along the highway at 30 miles an hour, never reaching its potential. This is Mr. Average Man. Another automobile not capable of doing more than 80 miles an hour is cruising down the highway at 70—it is realizing its optimum. This can be true of Mr. and Mrs. Average Christian. God indeed can make the "mostest out of the leastest" in and through the Holy Spirit. And it is our responsibility to be the very best for God, to turn all that he has given us, all that he has made us, all that he has provided for us, over to him to be used according to his will and to his glory.

Think of a poor, uneducated, terribly limited girl, working in a factory in Scotland. God picked her up, and she became the famous Mary Slessor of Calabar. One could cite a hundred instances of this sort. True in the past, true today, it can be true of you and me. God does not expect us to be what we are not, but he wants to enable us to be one hundred per cent of what we are and to perform to the limit of our abilities in the power of the Holy Spirit.

Whatever God asks us to do, he will provide sufficient power, strength, understanding and enablement for us to fulfill the task. The realization of this goal, however, hinges on our acceptance of God's will; on our laying aside our own personal, private desires, our small ambitions and longings; on our having complete confidence in God's love and his desire that we should be the very best in this life and for eternity.

Some time ago I met a serviceman who had made the army his career. I asked him why. His answer was this, "Uncle Sam provides for my every need: I have comfortable quarters, good clothes, excellent food, sufficient money, problems of accident and sickness. are taken care of. I have no problems with doctors' bills and hospital bills. I have no concern about my old age. I have security."

Possibly this was the answer of a man without much drive and ambition, but such earthly security can also be ours as Christians. God has told us we are not to make the three basic needs of physical life, namely, the need for food, clothing and shelter, a matter of concern, anxiety or ambition. He has promised that if we seek first his kingdom and his righteousness, he will provide these things. Naturally, these will be provided through the work that we do. The average man, either primitive or sophisticated, in the final analysis gives his strength in order to provide a minimum, or an affluent maximum, of food, clothing and shelter. God says this is not to be our goal, but rather himself and his kingdom and his righteousness. God then will see that we have adequate food, clothing and shelter. Our earthly security is thus in Christ.

In our quest for identity in an impersonal civilization is there anything more reassuring than the fact that God deals with us not in the mass but as individuals? My personhood is enhanced, not obliterated, as I live with God. "He calls his own sheep by name." God knows all that I am or am not. He accepts me as such. He loves me and desires more ardently than I do my self-realization and self-expression under his holy will and purpose. He calls me to "the courage to be" according to his Word and his Spirit. Only as I accept myself according to his will, can I be a real person. In all of this he promises me his strength and guidance.

There is one more element in our finding peace and total security in God, and that is the acceptance of ourselves and of God's will, which the Bible describes as "good and perfect." If I can accept myself as God accepts me, if I can believe God's promise that he will provide for my every need inwardly and outwardly, if I can accept God's will for my life, including his glorious, ultimate goal for me, my predestination to become like Christ, then I not only have peace with God, but I have the peace of God flooding my heart and life and surrounding me moment by moment, day by day. If, however, I am discontented, murmuring, grumbling, wishing I were somebody other than I am, wishing I had abilities I do not have, wishing I had a personality like someone else's, then I shall neither have the peace of God in my life day by day nor will God be fully realizing his will for me in this life on earth.

Remember God made us; we did not make ourselves. In the final analysis that initial deposit of what we are in personality, intelligence, body, appearance and all the rest is God's responsibility. But how I employ what I am and what God gives to me is my responsibility. I can either hide this sum total in a napkin and bury it in the ground, as did the man with one talent, or I can accept myself as God's child, loved by him as much as he loves anyone else, and invest my time and strength in the fulfillment of his will for me and for his kingdom. Then I shall be like the man with the five talents, which he turned into ten. And one day I shall hear my Lord say to me, "Well done! I made you as you are. You used to the optimum all I made you and all I gave you in the power of the Holy Spirit. Well done, good and faithful servant. Enter into the joy of your Lord. Enter into the joy of my reward for you."

Date Due
